1st edn '91   £5.00

D0177731

THE
SHELL BOOK
OF THE SHORE

THE
SHELL BOOK
OF THE SHORE

Tony Soper

Illustrations by Maggie Raynor

DAVID & CHARLES
Newton Abbot · London

Other books by Tony Soper

The Bird Table Book
Owls (with John Sparks)
Penguins (with John Sparks)
Birdwatch
A Passion for Birds
Oceans of Birds

Page 1 Peregrine

Page 2 Hermit crabs are soft-shelled by nature, protecting
themselves by hiding inside the borrowed shell of a snail – in
this case a common welk (*Heather Angel*)

British Library Cataloguing in Publication Data
Soper, Tony
The Shell book of the shore.
1. Organisms. Shells
I. Title
574.90946

ISBN 0–7153–9465–7

Typeset by ABM Typographics Ltd, Hull
and printed in Portugal
by Resopal
David & Charles plc
Brunel House   Newton Abbot   Devon

Contents

Foreword

If you are good at it, you can make a living from the seashore, eating fish soup, sea beet and cockles, and picking up lost coinage and diamond rings, not to mention pieces-of-eight, to pay for your visits to civilisation. But most of us go for fun, and because we never know what might be round the next corner. In some parts of the country it is in the blood, and men have actually come to blows in the struggle to be first into a promising cave as the tide falls back. Some get up before dawn to be first on the tideline; some do it the lazy way and drive a Land-Rover from end to end of the beach in a few minutes, making a lot of noise in the process.

Jellyfish, pit props, fish-boxes and far-flung timber riddled with shipworm and covered with goose barnacles; the list of possibilities is endless, including everything from a tropical bean to a barrel of rum. The seashore is the most rewarding of all habitats.

Oystercatchers and grey plover on a winter beach (*Roger Tidman/FLPA*)

1
Waves, Tides and Currents

The seashore belongs to us all – or at least, we like to think it does. In fact, well over a quarter of the 2,750 miles of coastline in England and Wales is already built up in one way or the other. Less than a quarter of it is 'protected' by nature reserves and the like, and almost all of it belongs to the Crown.

Of course, the coast has a very long history of settlement, but only relatively recently have people regarded it as a place of pilgrimage and pleasure. Until the seventeenth century fishermen had it pretty much to themselves. The first to discover its pleasure potential were those who journeyed to the coastal spas to indulge in sea bathing for the good of their health, only to discover that they enjoyed the convivial company and the splash of the waves.

Coastal resorts catered first for the gentry, then, with the arrival of the railway, for the tripping masses. Soon the visitors discovered the joys of the rock pool, and entered with gusto into the age of 'collecting'. The sea-plants and sea-creatures fascinated the Victorians, as they fascinate anyone who casts so much as a careless glance in their direction.

Those who started to use the coast as a 'resort' became very much aware of the charm of the place. Unlike the fishermen, whose cottages were built with their backs to the sea and who cursed when gales kept them ashore with empty bellies, the newcomers built houses with bay windows and balconies facing the sea, so that they could enjoy and marvel at its moods. For one of the great appeals of the seashore is its quality of constant change. Watching a sharp horizon blur as a squall approaches, sweeping aside brighter skies, is unmatched by any change of mood ashore. Seeing a calm blue sea turn slate grey and sprout white horses on its mounting waves is to gain a true insight into the power of old 'earth shaker'.

The changes in colour and movement of the sea are all gloriously unpredictable, depending on the weather, but one kind of change can be predicted fairly accurately, and that is the tide. The rhythm of the tide must form the framework for any exploration of the seaside, and a rough understanding of its nature is essential for real enjoyment of shore-going. You will need to look at tidal information in the local paper, or glean it from the radio, but best of all buy a copy of the tide-tables for your chosen port. For every day of the year your tide-table will list the times of high water and low water, and the heights to which these tides will rise or fall. Weather conditions may modify the figures (very high pressure, for example, will prevent the tide from rising to its predicted height), but it is possible to pinpoint these times and levels because they are under the control of a very predictable body – the moon.

The earth and the moon have a gravitational attraction for each other, and the force is exerted in a straight line between the two bodies. The nearer a place is to the moon, the stronger will be the pull of gravity. When gravity acts on the great mass of water in the oceans, it has the effect of 'sucking it up' in the direction of the gravitational pull. The effect of this 'sucking up' of the water is to produce two 'bulges' of water, a large one in areas of the earth closest to the moon, producing a higher tidal range, and a smaller one on the opposite side of the earth producing a lower tidal range.

As the earth spins on its axis once a day, most places in Britain experience two high and two low water periods every twenty-four hours, the high tides occuring whenever Britain is situated 'under' one of these two bulges. Between these peaks and troughs the water rises for approximately six hours from low water to high water (flooding) and falls for the same period ('ebbing'), until it reaches low water. The difference in height between these two levels is known as the 'range' of the tide. As the tide rises and falls, water is being moved from one part of the coast to another creating a 'tidal current', which is the result of the difference in height between the two places. In the English Channel, for example, the current during flood tide is always from west to east, since the time of high water is pro-

Flatfish, like this plaice, have cryptic
coloration which allows them to merge
into their background (*Heather Angel*)

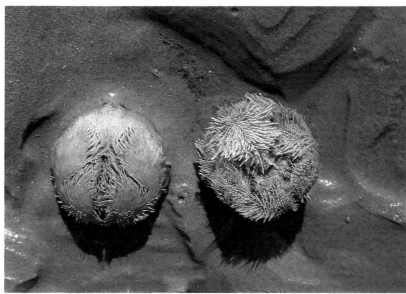

The sea potato, or heart urchin, burrows under the sand for safety (left-upper surface, right-underside); the empty skeleton or 'test' is often found on the shore (*Heather Angel*)

Oarweed and thongweed are only exposed to the air at the lowest of spring tides (*Heather Angel*)

gressively later as you travel eastwards. These currents may sometimes be very powerful, forming rips and tide-races, depending on the configuration of the coastline, and where they impinge on the beach itself they will affect the plants and animals that live there.

Another important aspect of the change between high and low water is the uneven rate of the rise and fall during the passage of the tide. When the tide is flooding, the first third of the rise takes two hours, the second third takes only one hour, while the last third takes three hours to rise. When the tide is ebbing the situation is reversed and it takes three hours to fall the first third, again one hour for the second third and two hours for the third. So in the middle range, whether the tide is ebbing or flooding, the speed of change is at its greatest. This is valuable information, allowing you to work out how much time you have to explore the low water ledges, and when to leave your private bay to avoid being cut off by the tide.

How high the tide will rise and how low it will fall depend upon the phases of the moon. At new and full moon, when the earth, the moon and the sun lie in a straight line and the effect of gravity is at its greatest, the tides, known as 'springs', will have their greatest range, producing the highest high tides and the lowest low tides. For the seven days following each new or full moon, the three heavenly bodies gradually move out of alignment until the sun and the moon lie at right-angles to the earth, when the effect of gravity is least. Now the tides are known as 'neaps', and they rise less and fall the least. Between neaps and springs the range gradually builds up and then down again every seven days, thus 'making' and 'taking off'. As the tide builds towards springs, each successive strandline will be removed, so that the receding water leaves just one strand of debris across the beach. As they take off, especially if conditions are calm and stable, the debris of each successive tide will remain, leaving several strandlines of current-borne debris for the diligent beachcomber to explore.

Twice a year, at the spring and autumn equinox, when in response to the rhythm of the sun's annual orbit of the earth, the earth, moon and sun achieve their most perfect linear alignment, the equinoctial spring tides occur, and the coast suffers its greatest tidal inundation as well as its lowest tides. These equinoctial springs occur about 21 March and 21 September each year, and the excitement comes at the low water period when plants, animals, submerged seaweed forests or ancient wrecks that normally lie below the surface are exposed to the air and are open for inspection. Whether these low water bonanzas occur at night or during daylight hours depends on which part of the country you are in, but darkness need be no deterrant. A torch-lit expedition to the lowest parts of the shore has its own excitement.

Weather conditions have quite significant effects on the height of the tide. Extremes of atmospheric pressure or strong steady winds may lower or raise the predicted height by as much as a third of a metre – a foot, for those who still think in the imperial measurement. Winds may advance or delay the actual time of high water as compared with predicted time. This effect is most noticeable in any kind of bottleneck; for example an estuary, where high water may be sustained by as much as an hour when an onshore wind holds the sea high up. Wind raises sea-level in the direction it is blowing, so a strong wind blowing directly onshore will pile up the water and cause sea-levels higher than predicted.

A low atmospheric pressure will tend to raise sea-level and a high pressure will depress it. A change of an inch (25mm) in the barometer reading indicates a variation of about a foot (30cm) in the height of sea-level, and that is about as great a change as is ever likely.

In the southern part of the North Sea, storm surges may cause tides to vary as much as more than 3ft or a metre from predicted heights, and even greater variations may occur in the Thames estuary. These surges are usually caused by deep depressions moving east across the northern part of the North Sea; they are the result of an oscillating effect by rapid changes of weather. In other parts of Great Britain this oscillating effect on sea-level produces a wave effect known as a seiche. This may have a height of anything from 1in to 3ft 3in (25mm to a metre) and the period between waves may be anything between a few minutes and a couple of hours. Small seiches are not uncommon, especially in certain harbours, for instance Fishguard and Wick, but they can cause a great deal of damage when they are unexpected.

Weather information is really important to the intending beachcomber, and it is as well to know your local sources. Meteorological offices give excellent short-term forecasts by telephone; you can find the number in the opening pages of the telephone directory. The BBC coastal waters' forecasts are useful, and offers both national and regional forecasts.

If you want to try your hand at your own weather forecasting you will need a barometer. But remember that single readings are not of much value. It is no good giving it a knowing tap as you walk out of the door, because unless you

WAVES, TIDES AND CURRENTS

Overleaf
The receding tide leaves a strandline of natural and unnatural debris which is the beachcombers delight (*Tony Soper*)

Inset
Storm-tossed razorshells, mussel shells and tube worms (*Tony Soper*)

BEAUFORT WIND SCALE

Beaufort wind force	Mean wind speed in knots	Descriptive terms	Sea criterion	Probable height of waves in feet/metres
0	less than 1	calm	Sea like a mirror.	—
1	1–3	light air	Ripples with the appearance of scales are formed but without foam crests.	1/4/.076
2	4–6	light breeze	Small wavelets, still short but more pronounced. Crests have a glassy appearance and do not break.	1/2/.152
3	7–10	gentle breeze	Large wavelets. Crests begin to break. Foam of glassy appearance. Perhaps scattered white horses.	2/.6
4	11–16	moderate breeze	Small waves, becoming longer. Fairly frequent white horses.	3 1/2/1.07
5	17–21	fresh breeze	Moderate waves, taking a more pronounced long form. Many white horses formed. (Chance of some spray.)	6/1.8
6	22–27	strong breeze	Large waves begin to form. White foam crests more extensive everywhere. (Probably some spray.)	9 1/2/2.9
7	28–33	near gale	Sea heaps up and white foam from breaking waves begins to be blown in streaks along the direction of the wind.	13 1/2/4.1
8	34–40	gale	Moderately high waves of greater length. Edges of crests begin to break into spindrift. The foam is blown in well-marked streaks along the direction of the wind.	18/5.5
9	41–47	strong gale	High waves. Dense streaks of foam along the direction of the wind. Crests of waves begin to topple, tumble and roll over. Spray may affect visibility.	23/7
10	48–55	storm	Very high waves with long overhanging crests. The resulting foam in great patches is blown in dense white streaks along the direction of the wind. On the whole the surface of the sea takes a white appearance. The tumbling of the sea becomes heavy and shocklike. Visibility affected.	29/8.8
11	56–63	violent storm	Exceptionally high waves. (Small and medium-sized ships might be for a time lost to view behind the waves.) The sea is completely covered with long white patches of foam lying along the direction of the wind. Everywhere the edges of the wave crests are blown into froth. Visibility affected.	37/11.3
12	64+	hurricane	The air is filled with foam and spray. Sea completely white with driving spray. Visibility very seriously affected.	45/13.7

have been giving it a whole series of knowing taps you will not know what the trend is. Weather forecasting with a barometer is nothing if it's not trendy!

The arrival of a gale is often forecast by a fall of pressure and by the wind backing (ie changing direction anti-clockwise). The actual change of pressure may be a fairly rapid progress, but the gale itself may be delayed a considerable time after the barometer indication. Steady or rising pressure when the pressure is already high is a likely indicator of quiet weather. Even if there are high winds at this time, they are unlikely to arrive suddenly; they will gradually increase in strength. After unsettled weather, a rising barometer probably forecasts better conditions.

It is very easy to make a crude 'beach barometer', but while it is an amusing thing to have, its forecasting value is not great. First, as Mrs Beeton would say, catch yourself a chianti bottle. Tear off the straw basket so that you're left with the naked bottle (and, incidentally, a red chianti bottle is more suitable than a white wine one). Now you need a Kilner jar. Fill the jar with water. Invert the empty (and clean and dry) chianti bottle and fit it into the Kilner jar. Take out water from the Kilner jar until the water comes up to cover the thick part (where the cork used to be) of the chianti bottle. The device, which is pressure controlled and depends on the locked air contained in the upturned bottle, may take several days to settle down. But, in due course, you will be able to observe atmospheric pressure changes indicated by the rising and falling of the water-level inside the neck of the wine bottle. Keep it away from direct sunlight and in ordinary room temperature.

The higher the water rises in the neck of the bottle, the better the weather will be. When the top of the bottle gets steamy, mist or light rain is due; and when the top gets full of condensation, it foretells heavy rain. Sometimes the water in the neck of the bottle is 'blown' out, and a heavy storm is imminent.

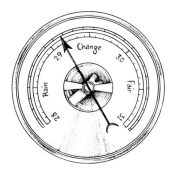

Stranded sperm whale on a beach, Orkney (*Peter Reynolds/FLPA*)

The egg-case of a dogfish is lashed to a frond of bladder wrack (*Heather Angel*)

In life the cowries (left-common, right-arctic) forage over weedy stones; their empty shells are cast onto the open beach in due course (*Heather Angel*)

WAVES, TIDES AND CURRENTS

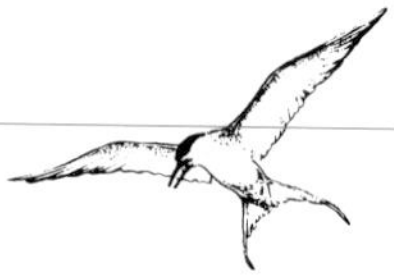

To go with your home-made barometer, you might like to remember the old seamen's rhymes, which are good advice, nine times out of ten:

> Long foretold, long last,
> Short notice, soon past,
> Quick rise after low,
> Sure sign of stronger blow.

> When the glass falls low
> prepare for a blow;
> When it slowly rises high,
> lofty canvas you may fly.

> At sea with low and falling glass,
> Soundly sleeps a careless ass,
> Only when it's high and rising,
> Truly rests a careful wise one.

> The evening red and morning grey
> Are sure signs of a fine day,
> But the evening grey and the morning red,
> Makes the sailor shake his head.

> Mackerel sky and mares' tails,
> Make lofty ships carry low sails.

The traditional piece of weather-forecasting seaweed offers a crude measure of humidity. When the seaweed becomes damp, rain is imminent. But, sadly, it's not a very reliable forecaster. If you want to try it, then the right species of kelp to use is *Laminaria saccharina,* the one with a long (anything up to 8ft (2.5m) undivided wavy frond, yellowy olive with a smooth cylindrical stalk and attached to stones and rocks by the root-like structures of a holdfast.

Currents and tidal streams are phenomena of enormous interest to the beachcomber. A knowledge of the local surface movements of the sea water and the way in which they relate to ocean currents is vital when stating with any certainty where 'wreck' has come from, and even more importantly, where it is likely to be cast ashore, in prevailing weather conditions.

Sea water expands and contracts in seasonal cycles. Along with the effect of constant winds, this results in ocean movements. Their direction is influenced by the earth's

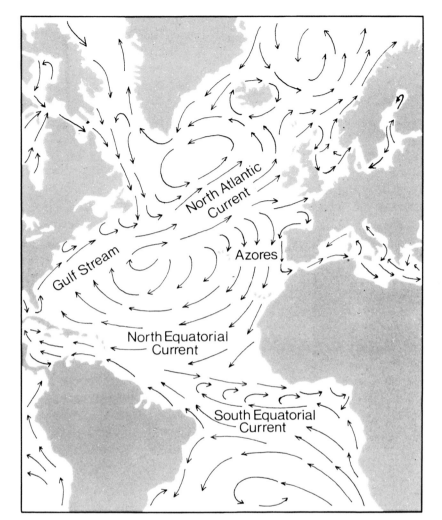

Chart showing surface current circulation in the North Atlantic; tropical beans unfortunate enough to fall into the Caribbean sea may find themselves cast ashore in Western Europe (*The chart is based on BA Chart No 5310 with the sanction of the Controller, HM Stationery Office and of the Hydrographer of the Navy*)

rotation; and in the northern hemisphere the general circulation is in a clockwork direction (like the whirlpool in your bath). In the North Atlantic this sea-current revolves round the Azores' 'High', the more or less permanent anti-cyclone system. And the result (which is of immense importance to all beachcombers) is that the Gulf Stream, of tropical origin, works its way up the eastern seaboard of North America, then travels east across the Atlantic to become the North Atlantic Current, losing strength and splitting into two parts, one flowing northwards past Scotland and the other eastwards to the English Channel and the Bay of Biscay. Now you know why it is that Caribbean plant seeds sometimes end up on west-coast beaches – and sometimes great quantities of pelagic jellyfish.

Changes in wind speed and direction alter the nature of this

Overleaf
Common seals breed on tidal sandbanks around the coast of East Anglia, but often in more exposed areas round the Scottish coasts (*Leo Batten/FLPA*)

great current, and the resulting maverick movements are known as the North Atlantic Drift. In coastal waters local currents are influenced by the effects of rain, tidal streams and the local geography.

Charting the course of these currents has involved the release of many thousands of drift bottles and, more recently, plastic drift envelopes. They are used by organisations interested in currents and tides. For instance, the Ministry of Agriculture, Fisheries and Food and the Marine Biological Association want to know about plankton and fish movements in relation to sea movements; and industrialists wish to trace the likely course of effluent and chemical waste when it is dumped at sea.

The National Institute of Oceanography once organised a massive drop of plastic drift envelopes. Aircraft of Royal Air Force Command released some 9,000 envelopes between the Bay of Biscay and the Faeroes. The heavy plastic envelopes contained postcards requesting information about date and recovery position. Previous experience in Australian and South African waters had shown that these surface-drifters were susceptible to attack by albatross and other seabirds. So in this experiment a thin sheet of cork was enclosed with the postcard, to give added buoyancy. The cards were dropped in bundles of ten, loosely bound with a disintegrating tape, at four and a half minute intervals, that is, every 10 miles (16km) along the track. A reward was offered to the finder.

The results were highly successful. Eighteen months after the drop more than 2,500 cards had been returned to the Institute, representing a 40 per cent recovery rate. The envelopes were returned by beachcombers working the coasts between southern Portugal and northern Scandinavia. Some of the cards were fresh and clean, some were dog-eared and faded, some pulped and almost unreadable – yet of all the cards returned, only one was so disintegrated that the vital serial number was unreadable.

One thousand three hundred and twenty-seven of the cards beached on the shores of the British Isles, twice as many as on the other coasts. This result was not surprising, but it confirmed the expected effect of the North Atlantic Drift. More than half of the British cards were returned from the remoter parts of the Scottish Islands, over 200 of them coming from Shetland. None at all was found between the Firth of Forth and the Thames estuary, and only a few from the north west, a result which showed, not surprisingly, that those stretches of coastline are relatively unaffected by ocean currents. Three of the cards were

retrieved from Portugal, but the most exciting recovery was of a card which had travelled all the way to the Rybachi Peninsula in the Barents Sea, just inside the Russian border.

The experiments showed that floating objects in the sea area off the British Isles between Biscay and the Faeroes tend to strand somewhere on the shores of north-west Europe, influenced by prevailing wind conditions, and that the odds are very much in favour of such objects landing on British or Irish beaches. It is clear that wind conditions are very important in predicting the course made good by floating 'wreck'.

Surface ocean currents are mirrored by underwater currents, which are normally on a reciprocal course, and some drift devices are designed to plot underwater currents in much the same way that surface currents are traced. But such a device, since it must first sink and then jog along the sea bed, looks rather different from the simple postcard in the envelope. Much of the current seabed research has taken place in the southern North Sea, using specially weighted glass bottles. But nowadays the favoured transport is the 'Woodhead sea-bed drifter', a gaily-coloured plastic mushroom, with a $\frac{1}{4}$oz (7g) copper weight crimped to the bottom of its stalk.

In much the same way as the plastic surface-drift envelopes, the sea-bed drifters are released in bundles, tied with a soluble film attached to a bag of gravel. When the film dissolves after about 20 minutes, the saucer mushrooms stand up and drift off wherever the current takes them. A numbered polythene tag is attached to the saucer, with the legend 'reward for drifter, tag and full details'. On the saucer itself is an embossed message in several languages, asking the finder to inform his Fishery Officer, or the Fisheries Laboratory at Lowestoft. Many of the drifters are caught in trawl nets, but many of them escape capture this way and end up on beaches. The recovery rate is very satisfactory. Of 2,000 drifters released south of the Dogger Bank, 48 per cent had been returned within one year; 11 per cent of these came from beaches. Subsequent experiments have confirmed the same pattern.

Woodhead sea-bed drifters

Success with these investigations obviously depends a great deal on the co-operation of both fishermen and beachcombers, but it is not surprising that people are willing to go to the small trouble of returning a drifter; there is a sense of romance and mystery about these frail objects, carrying their tell-tale number-tag – the key to information about their wanderings. And, of course, there is often a reward!

The practice of sealing messages into a bottle and casting it to the sea in the hope that someone somewhere will recover it is

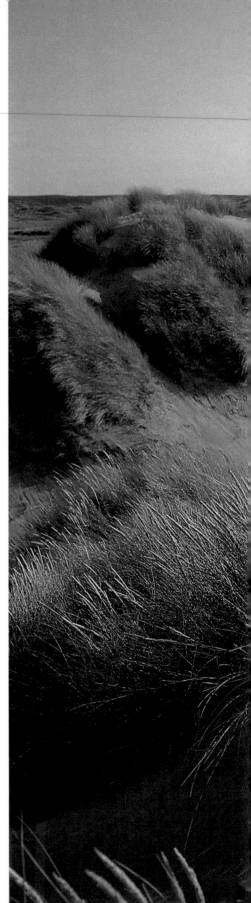

Some plants such as sea holly and marram grass are pioneers in the process of stabilising sand dunes (*Heather Angel*)

Sand dunes are the perfect playground, but they are vulnerable to 'blow-outs' if they are trodden by too many feet (*Heather Angel*)

very long established. Not only serious oceanographers use the sea-post. It is not easy to be sure when the custom began. Certainly the British ship *Rainbow* put out floating bottles in 1802 to test currents, but continental researchers put the date as early as 1763; these dates relate to the scientific use of bottle-post. Bernardin de Saint-Pierre, writing in 1784, claims that Christopher Columbus, when in danger of perishing in the mid-Atlantic tempest, consigned an account of his discoveries to a barrel which he committed to the waves in the hope that it would arrive sooner or later on a beach.

Following a boatman's discovery of a vital political secret (that Novya Zemblya had been seized from Russia by the Dutch) contained in a bottle message picked up on the beach at Dover, Queen Elizabeth in 1560 appointed an official Uncorker of Bottles. Any unauthorised person who let his curiosity get the better of him in the matter of opening stranded messenger bottles was liable to hang. The Crown appointment lapsed in the reign of George III; just as well perhaps.

In the mid-nineteenth century it was common for floating bottles with papers inside to be flung overboard from outward-bound emigrant ships.

The practice of using drift bottles and other buoyant message containers for serious oceanographic research is long-established and still going strong today. An empty bottle will drift largely under the influence of wind and, to determine surface sea currents, the bottle is ballasted with a carefully calculated amount of sand. Usually there is also a questionnaire postcard printed in several languages, an information slip and an easily-seen label asking the finder to break the bottle and take the first step towards his reward. One side of the card is printed with a return address. If all the questions are answered, then the researcher will know where and when a bottle began and ended its journey. Time actually spent afloat is not so easily determined because, of course, a bottle may have lain on the beach undiscovered for some time. But, over a period of time, it is possible to make a fairly accurate assessment. Finders of British bottles get a small reward, and the satisfaction of having done their bit towards ocean research. Over the years, drift experiments have done a great deal towards establishing the pattern of surface and bottom movements. For instance, Dr Fulton's research in the years 1894–7, for the Fishery Board of Scotland, established the existence of a great cyclonic surface-current system in the North Sea.

Over the years a surprising variety of message-carrying floaters has been used – barrels, cylinders, spheres, buoys, tubes, etc, and even coconut shells. Very often bottles and envelopes have been retrieved by fishermen while they were still at sea. Records like this are very useful in filling the gaps and giving more information about the path the bottles are following on their way to shore.

Sometimes bottles travel great distances and wait long periods for discovery. One was released by Dr W. S. Bruce of the Scottish Antartic Expedition of 1902–4, in the Southern Ocean, east of Cape Horn, to be discovered fifty years later lying on a sand dune on the North Island of New Zealand, a journey of some 10,000 miles (16,000km). A message-containing barrel released by the American Admiral Melville near Cape Barrow in Alaska in September 1899, was recovered on the north coast of Iceland about six years later, having travelled at least 2,500 miles (4,000km) and being 'out' for 2,092 days.

At one time the Board of Admiralty ordered all HM ships to take part in bottle-post experiments, and the necessary printed paper was available for requisition through RN Stores. It was a common thing for bottle messages to request finders to pass details to Lloyds.

There have been many records of west-to-east journeys across the Atlantic in middle and higher latitudes, and east-to-west travels in low latitudes. The eastward journey from New York waters to France and the Iberian Peninsula takes an average of 550 days.

Not all messages are of a scientific or navigational nature. In 1842 the brig *Superior*, an emigrant vessel commanded by Donald Mansen, was on passage from Thurso to Quebec. At the position 53° 48′N, 24°W she released the bottle message 'This morning a male child was born; mother and infant are in a fair way and passengers are all in a healthy state'. In due course this bottle covered 1,500 sea miles and stranded on a beach within 2 miles of Thurso, the ship's departure point.

The cases where bottle-post has been used in real disaster are not so easy to track down, but no doubt they've occurred often enough. In July 1884, some fishermen picked up a distress message which seems likely to have been genuine. The bottle was found stranded in Morecambe Bay; the message stated that the crew of the vessel *Himalaya* saw death ahead of them. The ship's sails had been blown away, the propeller was broken, the hull was holed; she had been cast on the rocks near to Newfoundland, and Captain Roberts and his crew of sixteen were on the point of drowning. 'There is nothing we can do to save ourselves', read the message, 'if God does not intervene with a miracle we shall perish'. The note was signed 'J. Roberts,

Terns breed in colonies in amongst
sand dunes, then plunge-dive for sand-
eels at the very edge of the sea
(*D. Pearce/FLPA*)

Right
Saltmarsh plants are hardy specimens,
adapted to a life alternating between
exposure to open air and inundation
by salt water, to say nothing of
occasional rain; glasswort, sea
purslane, sea lavender and cord-grass
(*Heather Angel*)

Far right
Low water on the Mawddach estuary
reveals the complex pattern of mud-
banks and channels; prime feeding
areas for wading birds and a foothold
for pioneer plants (*Heather Angel*)

Captain'. Nothing more was heard of the vessel or crew.

In 1949 a distress message, which was certainly genuine, was found in a bottle which had been released forty-five years earlier by the polar explorer Evelyn Baldwin. He had scribbled a hasty note calling for aid, had enclosed it in a small water-tight container, and cast it into the Arctic Ocean. The message drifted and remained undiscovered for nearly half a century until a Soviet fisherman discovered it in the sea ice in the Russian Arctic. The note, written in Norwegian and English read: 'Five ponies and 150 dogs remaining. Desire hay, fish and 30 sledges. Must return early in August. Baldwin'. In fact, although the message arrived forty-five years too late, the expedition returned safely; Baldwin died a natural death at his home in 1933.

Bottle-post has been used by evangelists to carry the Word; by distillers to promote their taste; and by broadcasters to publicise their products. A bottle was set adrift outside New York harbour by the sponsors of a radio programme with a note inside offering the reward of $1,000 to the finder. It was not a hoax and after a 2,500-mile passage the reward was successfully claimed by an Azorean boy. A bottle found in 1942 contained a message from the skipper of a launch which had been lost seven months earlier. It contained a valid will written on the back of a blank cheque. An American bachelor consigned to the sea fifteen copies of a proposal in fifteen sealed bottles. In due course he received four acceptances. Years ago the organisers of the Irish Sweepstake produced a bottle, shaped like a fish, containing a leaflet with information and the Dublin address from which sweepstake tickets were available. The most attractive part of this scheme was a credit note for £1 when presented to the landlord of the local inn.

Drift bottles are, however, above all, a scientific proposition, and one of the most romantic of research techniques. So it is appropriate to leave them with a reference to Alfred de Vigny's poem 'La Bouteille à la Mer'. He relates that, in 1842, a bottle was thrown out in the open sea with a label 'catch me who can'. After many vicissitudes, it is retrieved by a young fisherman who straightaway takes his precious find to a wise man, demanding to be told the nature of the elixir within it. The answer comes in ringing tones: 'Quel est cet elixir! Pêcheur, c'est la Science'.

So, in the interests of science, I want to put in a word against the silly practice of sending false messages to sea in a bottle-boat. There are too many records of bottles that have been consigned to the sea carrying messages of non-existent distress and every kind of hoax. In the light of known existence of genuine emergency messages these are clearly only for the feeble-minded. The bare record of date and position confided to a bottle securely corked and sealed and ballasted to float with minimum freeboard, offers a prospect far more practical and exciting than jolly jokes about castaways on desert islands. But do not forget to include your name and address.

The currents, which have been so effectively charted by drift devices over the years, eventually carry their flotsam to a beach, and the action of sea water on the beach itself is of absorbing interest. For the material of the beach, whether it is small particles of sand or large pebbles, is constantly on the move.

In mythology, Zeus or Neptune, the god of the sea, was also known as Earth-shaker, a much-deserved name. The pounding force of a wave on the beach may be as much as 6½ tons per square foot (70 tonnes per square metre). It is no wonder that the living creatures inhabiting these regions are specially designed to withstand pressure. In winter storms, granite blocks are torn from seaside promenades, and the sea hurls pebbles and boulders at the cliffs. We may call the seashore a battle ground, but it is as well to concede that the sea is the greater force and that it calls the tune to which the land dances.

Waves are formed by wind pressure, which causes the sea to undulate into ridges of water – crests separated by troughs – that drive along at a slight angle from the direction of the wind. The stronger the wind, the greater the waves, but the size of them is affected very much by the 'fetch' of sea – the uninterrupted distance over which the wind has play. In sheltered waters a severe wind will only raise a short chop, whereas in open sea the same wind will produce violent effects.

In shallow waters, for instance, when a wave approaches the shore and is affected by friction with the sea bed, it changes its character, becoming shorter and with a steepening slope, until it eventually topples over. After breaking, it goes back to sea again, creating an undertow beneath the next advancing wave.

There is a scouring action along the shoreline, in which, generally speaking, the bigger the wave the greater the movement. Large waves tend to move the larger pebbles the greatest distance, small waves move the smaller particles. And it seems that for a particular size of wave there is a particular size of material that moves at the greatest rate. However, waves rarely hit a beach exactly square on, and their oblique arrival causes beach pebbles to be displaced either one way or the other along the beach. These findings were confirmed by research

geologists who traced the movements of individual pebbles by marking them with marine paint and then following their progress day by day over a period of weeks. Other marking techniques include the use of radio-active isotopes, acoustic pebbles and fluorescent dyes.

So the character of the beach is shaped by the wind-formed waves that pound or play against it. The strength of the wind and the fetch determine the size of those waves. Even a gentle breeze may produce large waves, provided the fetch covers hundreds or thousands of miles. A 10-knot breeze may produce 5ft (1.5m) waves and these waves may continue long after their formation wind has died; in these conditions we have what is called a groundswell. Now a submerged and un-obstructed pebble of 5in (10cm) diameter will be moved by water travelling at 2 knots. Smooth stones of 2 to 3in (5 to 7.5cm) diameter may be shifted on a shingle beach by water travelling at 4 knots. If the pebbles are too large to move, then the sea batters at them until they become small enough. The motion of the sea tends to distribute the beach material in an even layer, and it constantly exerts a grading motion. Since it's easier to move downhill, there is a tendency for pebbles to move away offshore.

In a storm, the sea will pick up pebbles and stones and hurl them at the cliffs. Over a period of time, the cliffs are reduced to beach material, forming a ridge, a storm beach.

There are, of course, other forces at work, such as frost, sun and rain, and their effects are not confined to times of heavy weather. The coast has a lot to contend with, and the foreshore is indeed a restless and dynamic piece of country. But not only does it move; it lives.

2

Golden Sand

In Britain it isn't possible to live more than 80 miles (128km) away from the coast, and since its 'discovery' the seaside has proved a magnet, drawing millions of holiday makers every year. The seaside is especially good for family holidays – something for everyone – and for the younger members in particular, the big attraction, apart from the water itself, is all that sand. Sand is fun wherever it is, but the big difference between the stuff in the sandpit and the sand on the beach is that the seaside version is somebody else's home.

The magical thing about those sand grains is that although they are individually so tough, and packed tightly against their neighbours, they are small enough to retain a coating of sea water around them by capillary action even during the period when the tide has retreated. This means that the sterile grinding action is so reduced that the beach is capable of supporting life. Above high-water mark, where the sand is dry, the rasping effect does occur and the habitat is correspondingly less fertile. Like the shingle beach, it is then only on the much higher level, where there is no wave action, that primitive plants can start their work of binding the dunes and making life possible for other species.

On a busy August bank holiday it may seem that people are the only animals on the beach, apart from a handful of raucous dogs and importunate gulls. But the sand is a jungle of wild creatures, if you know where to look. At high-water mark, for instance, there may be a ribbon development of dead plants, freshly thrown up by the receding tide, and this will support a thriving population of sand-hoppers – *Talitrus saltator* is the one

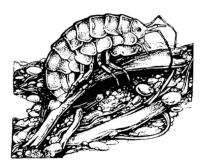

The sandhopper *Talitrus*, much enlarged

35

GOLDEN SAND

Turnstones are beach birds, living up to their name by turning stones and seaweed in search of edible debris and small animals

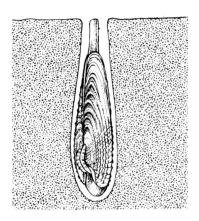

Piddocks bore into soft rock, then enlarge the burrow as they grow

most likely to be spotted — but there are over a thousand different species at large. During the day these 'sand fleas' live underground in the dry upper areas of the shore, but at night they come out, to leap about and hunt over the tide-line debris and the lower shore, scavenging decaying plant and animal material brought in by the tide.

A surprising number of birds will visit the shore to hunt these sand fleas, and to search among the tide-line debris for flies and molluscs. Turnstones are the most at home here, but pied wagtails and crows come in a close second, while many of the birds more commonly regarded as woodland and garden species will come to try their luck. Robins, blackbirds, starlings and sparrows all make successful visits to the shore.

On the earth nothing is new. Basic materials are used over and over again, re-appearing in different guises. Sand grains on the beach start life as part of a solid rock. That rock might be solid granite or gleaming chalk; or the wheel may turn full circle when sandstone, a rock made from compacted sand grains, is again broken down to its component parts. The sea, of course, is the giant that crushes rock into sand, but in the case of sandstone, or other soft substrates like shale, slate or chalk, the process of breakdown may be aided by molluscs which are, literally, boring. Several species do it — the common piddock is a good example.

In the larval stage of its life the piddock free-floats in the plankton but, settling on a suitably soft rock, it sets to work with its specially designed drilling shells. With a see-saw action and rotating the valves through a right-angle, rows of fine teeth bore into the rock. Quite a small hole is made, for the animal itself is small at this stage. But once inside and safe from predators, it grows, and in growing enlarges the chamber, until it may reach back a foot (30cm) into the rock. For the rest of its life it inhabits this self-made cave, reaching out to feed on passing titbits when the tide is in. When, in due course, it dies, the sea is able to reach an eroding finger into the little cavern and exploit it further, taking advantage of the weak spot engineered by the piddock.

There's no doubt that the principal demolition agency is the sea, when, in destructive vein, it acts directly on the rock of the land. At the base of cliffs, for example, waves may cut into the rock until an overhang is formed, and eventually rocks fall. This tumble of rocks is then pounded and crushed by the waves, so that boulders become large pebbles, then smaller pebbles, until they become small and light enough for the waves to pick up and carry away. During the journey from cliff

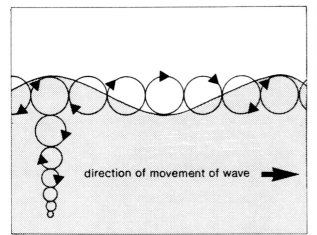 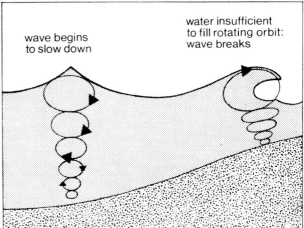

to beach resting-place, a lot of wear and tear goes on, so the
sand grains which survive to build our beaches need to be made
of pretty hard and enduring stuff.

Wave action

Waves, which are the most important agents in transporting
sand around the coast, are formed far out at sea by the action of
the wind. On the beach we see them in many different shapes
and sizes; as gentle ripples or crashing breakers as they expend
their energy on the shore. But in the open sea, they have a
circular form, developed as the wind drives individual particles
of water in oscillatory movements. The water particles move
round and round, without actually moving forward very
much; the orbits they perform have several different characteristics which, combined, account for the state of the sea on a
particular day. In deep water, the sea bed does not impinge on
the circular motions; even the highest waves of a stormy sea
leave the deep sea bed undisturbed. But as the swells approach
land and the water becomes shallower, the influence of the sea
bed becomes felt, so that the water particles that previously
moved in circular fashion take on an elliptical form, gradually
flattening towards the bottom, until at the sea bed itself the
movement is largely to and fro. This friction between the sea
bed and the moving water stirs up sediments lying offshore,
and thus the waves pick up their load. Sand that is raised from
the offshore banks is then carried by the moving waves; and
whether it is then deposited to form a sandy beach, or used like
a scouring powder by waves to erode yet more land, depends
largely upon the prevailing winds and the configuration of the
coast.

On a particular piece of coastline the wind, and therefore the
waves, approach most often from a particular direction. In the
south of England, for instance, the prevailing winds are south-

37

GOLDEN SAND

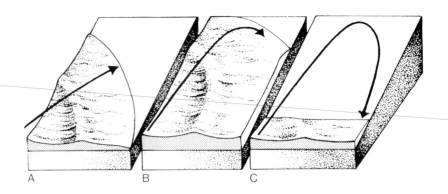

Longshore drift:
A Waves driven obliquely by wind and current against shore
B Debris swept up beach in a curve
C Wave subsides, material is dragged back and is thus carried along the coast in a zig-zag path

westerlies. They are responsible for moving beach materials in the general direction of west to east, by the all-important process known as 'longshore drift'. Longshore drift operates by virtue of the fact that waves usually approach the shore at an angle. The waves, with their cargo of sand, follow this diagonal line of approach up the beach – the action of 'swash'; but when the water of the 'backwash' returns to the sea, it naturally follows the line of least resistance and runs back at right-angles to the shore – straight down the beach. This kind of action, wave after wave, ensures that any beach material being carried is moved along – zig-zag fashion – in the direction of the prevailing wind and waves.

The balance of power between the swash and the backwash decides whether a beach is being built up or gradually removed. Out at sea, the speed of individual water particles is less than the speed of the wave as a whole, but as the wave is slowed down by contact with the sea bed the orbital velocity catches up until, at the crest, it is the same as the speed of the wave itself. The wave inevitably spills over, or breaks. Waves must break when they reach the shore, and it is the manner of this breaking which determines whether the wave will be 'constructive', with the swash most powerful, or 'destructive'. In calm conditions and in sheltered places waves spill over gently, pushing sand up the beach, and the energy of the backwash is soon dissipated by percolation through the sand and shingle. These are constructive waves. In storm conditions and on exposed coasts, when strong winds allow steep waves to develop, these reach the shore as plunging breakers which fall almost vertically on to the beach, producing a very strong backwash – the 'undertow' – which can be so dangerous to bathers. These waves are destructive.

Constructive waves are best for bathers, surfers in particular, who ride ashore by manipulating the wave energy for their own purpose. For the animals that live in the region of the beach it is clearly important that constructive waves should bring in sand to build their home environment, and the quality of the sand is also significant. The quality of the sand matters most to the inhabitants when the tide is out, because it is then that this unlikely medium must provide shelter, water, oxygen and food for worms and starfish, razorshells and cockles. For the animals, the stuff of which the sand is made – the inorganic rock – does not matter much, but the size of the particles does. Just like the terrestrial soil, the coarser the grains of sand the less they are able to hold water around themselves by capillary action. The swash and backwash of the waves achieves some grading of material on the beach, the larger, heavier particles being carried furthest up the beach while the weaker backwash drags back to the bottom only the finer sands and sediments. It is in these lower regions, where sand retains most moisture, that the greatest concentrations of animals are found.

The sandy beach is not an easy place in which to live, but there is a twice-daily delivery of fresh food, on each tidal inundation, and where there is an available food source you can depend on the ingenuity of animals to take advantage of it. There are various reasons why a hungry animal should not just sit on the beach and wait for dinner time. The heat of the sun, driving cold rain, the pounding force of the waves, and passing predators are just a few of them. But the effect of sun, wind and waves are only skin deep. If you can dig down just a little way you are in a relatively stable environment, with more or less constant salinity and temperature. So the most elegant way of avoiding these problems is to burrow under the sand during unfavourable periods, migrating up and down in order to feed or to hide. Burrowing animals have a choice of several ways of feeding. They may reach out and sample the passing plankton; they may scour the surface deposits left by the passage of the tides; they may sieve the goodness out of the sand itself; or they may hunt other burrowers. One way or another, then, the wet sand supports a vast community of worms, crustaceans, molluscs, echinoderms and burrowing fishers, each with its own particular method of feeding.

The lugworm is a good example, swallowing the sand it lives in, sorting and digesting the organic debris, and rejecting the inedible portion. Not surprisingly, it has a lot of material to reject, and this is thrown up on the surface in worm-like casts. These characteristic sand piles are easy to find when the tide is out, and are a sure indication that there is a lugworm underneath. They are often black, revealing the presence of a sulphide-rich layer in the sand, where most of the oxygen has been used up by the sand inhabitants. A few inches away from the sand cast there will be a shallow depression in the surface, and this marks the entrance to the worm's U-shaped gallery. When the tide comes in, it imports a fresh supply of sand and food particles which fill the depression,and the worm then gets to work swallowing it. If all goes well, the worm will remain in the same burrow for a long time, although it is an insubstantial construction, the walls stiffened with mucus. The worm itself is fat and juicy, and can be anything up to 8in (20cm) long. Fish certainly regard it as a prize, and that is why countless thousands of lugworms are dug up for use as bait by anglers every year.

The other marine worms that are very common on the lower reaches of a sandy beach are the tube worms, which build themselves a home out of the only material available to them, the sand itself. The 'sand mason' secretes a sticky mucus which is the binding material used in constructing a kind of sheath that allows the worm to move up and down in sympathy with the tidal rhythm. Down below, it has a measure of safety from the elements and its predators. Reaching up, when the tide is in, it can extend its tentacles and gills to collect food particles from the immediate area of its front door. When the tide recedes, only the top end of the sandy tube remains visible. Sometimes, after a storm, large numbers of the tubes may be wrenched from the sand and thrown up on the tide line. They are well worth examining closely, revealing the most painstaking efforts of the builder.

Another marvel of construction is the fragile 'shell' of the sea potato, or heart urchin *Echinocardium*, which is often found at the tide's edge after its owner has died. A white and rather skull-like capsule, the hollow skeleton (or test) is marked with five rows of holes from which, in life, emerged the hydraulic tube-feet of the animal. These five rays are characteristic of all the sea urchins and the closely related starfish. Hold the empty test up to the sky to see the full beauty of the radiating arms.

While the empty test is superficially similar to that of the edible urchin, *Echinus*, whose beautifully coloured globe is so sadly offered for sale by seaside shell shops, the life-style of the sea potato is very different. While *Echinus* grazes on rocks and seaweed, *Echinocardium* burrows in sand. To find it you must go to the lower shore at low water. Look, at the sort of places where lugworms advertise themselves so clearly, for a star-shaped depression in the sand. Find one with clear, recently-formed markings. Dig down gently with your fingers, anything up to 8in (20cm). Unlike the edible sea urchin, its spines are

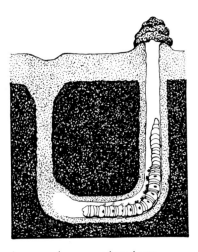

Lugworm burrow and sand cast

40

soft, almost furry, so there is no danger of pricking your fingers – but be gentle, it is only too easy to crush the shell.

Once you have the sandy coloured creature in your hands, have a close look at the spines. Some are spade-shaped – specially modified as digging tools. And notice that the spines are 'laid back' against the test, all facing the same way, as a further aid to burrowing. The five-rayed arrangement of holes in the test allows the tube feet to emerge and do their various jobs, helping with respiration, food collection and delivery and disposal of waste. Since the animal lives in its burrow a fair distance from the surface, some of the hydraulic tubes have to reach nearly 4in (10cm) by way of a chimney to search about for food particles. Put the urchin back into its burrow after you have examined it and cover it carefully with sand. If you simply leave it on the surface in the open air, it cannot burrow fast enough to escape marauding gulls. It takes perhaps fifteen minutes to burrow out of sight.

The burrowing starfish, *Astropecten,* is a close relative of the sea potato, although its starfish shape is superficially very different. But once you remember the five-rayed symmetry, which is typical of echinoderms, the relationship becomes more credible. *Astropecten* burrows down just beneath the surface, but maintains a surface presence with the tips of its arms. Instead of feeding on chance particles of food, it is an active predator, seizing small molluscs and swallowing them whole. Since the bivalve shellfish have to gape open at intervals, even when they are in someone else's stomach, the starfish waits its time, letting its digestive juices do their dirty work when the shell relaxes. In due course the central disc shows itself above the sand and rejects the cleaned-out shells.

A quite different process is used by the more familiar starfish of the rocky shore, *Asterias,* which uses its sucker feet to force open the mollusc shells, then protrudes its stomach into the shell to enjoy the starfish *in situ.* The burrowing starfish eats its meal in the secrecy of its sandy hideout, but in any case its tube feet are pointed for burrowing, and it would be hard put to clamber about on rocks the way *Asterias* does. *Astropecten* does not need to be covered after you have looked at it. Put it on wet soft sand, at low water. Its finger tips flex and probe. Slowly, it sinks below the surface as you watch, leaving a faintly outlined star in the sand to mark its lair.

The commonest of all shore animals are the molluscs, whose empty shells litter the surface of many beaches. One of the most successful of all animal groups, molluscs crawl, burrow, float and swim both by land and by sea all over the world, but the greatest concentrations of them live in the sand, out of sight, protected by their armour plating. Broadly speaking, the gastropod molluscs – the single-valved snails – live on rocky shores or on the seaweeds, and the under-sand creatures belong to a different class of animals, the *Bivalvia*. Bivalve molluscs live in sand, wood or rock (like the piddocks) or by mooring themselves to some sympathetic anchorage. Under the surface of a sandy beach they live in uncountable numbers. Indeed, one of the many remarkable features of molluscan life is the variety of methods they used to deal with different habitats, along with the astonishing populations they maintain. It is said that an acre of cockle flats in South Wales supports a million and a half cockles – that would be more than three and a half million to the hectare.

Yet molluscs are simple creatures. A bag of guts concentrated in a hump and attached to a muscle system which acts as a foot, the whole protected by a calcareous shell formed from a mantle of tissue. They come in all shapes and sizes, from those that creep behind your garden shed to giant squids, by way of cockles and mussels. Cockles are typical of extensive sand flats. Buried just beneath the surface when the tide comes in, they extend two siphons. Water enters through one, is sieved through the gills for the food particles suspended in it, then ejected through the other. The fat cockle feeds on minute plankton plants and suchlike titbits. It is customary for the gourmet cockle-eater to be told to keep the animal in salt water for a few hours while it rejects any grit or shell particles going through its system, but the longshore cocklers I've met scorn such niceties.

Cockles are harvested in enormous numbers, both by people and other animals. When the tide is in, they are hunted by starfish and flatfish. When the tide is out, the cockle-gatherers rake, scrape and dig for them, filling sacks which may be carried home on donkey back. In the Isles of Scilly I knew a farmer who took his horse and harrowed the low-water sand flats for cockles on occasion. In Morecambe Bay, apart from more conventional methods, cocklers are said to tread the sand with their bare feet, to persuade cockles to come to the surface. This is a technique also used by herring gulls. You often see them standing thoughtfully near the water's edge, then they deliberately stamp their feet, compacting the sand and forcing an uncomfortable worm or cockle to come up for air. But catching the cockle is only half the problem. The shell is thick and strong, the meat is armour-plated for protection. The gull has a simple, if crude, solution. He carries the cockle in his beak to

Herring gull 'puddling' for cockles

the nearest road or promenade, drops it from a height, then lands to claim the shattered prize.

The bird with the most advanced method for harvesting sea shells is the oystercatcher. In spite of its name, it mostly hunts cockles and mussels. One of the common shore and lower estuary waders, the black and white 'sea pie' is a familiar sight. And a familiar sound, too, for that matter, with its almost continuous piping and calling. But apart from the striking pied plumage, it has a powerful weapon in its long red beak. Most waders have delicate probing bills, but the oystercatcher is an exception. Its beak is the next best thing to a burglar's jemmy.

Patrolling the sand flats in an inch or two of water, the oystercatcher carries his head to one side, looking for the tell-tale open gape of a feeding cockle. If all goes well he can spear it before it senses danger and closes up. Then, most likely he will have severed the adductor muscle and the meat is laid out ready for eating. But even if the bivalve closes on the bird's beak, the oystercatcher is strong enough to force the two halves of the shell apart. If all else fails he has the capacity to penetrate the shell by brute force, with the chisel end of his beak. In the case of mussels, his other favourite dish, he uses somewhat similar methods, stalking the prey in the hope of catching it relaxed and unawares. But faced with a firmly closed shell, the bird turns the mussel over to reveal the flat ventral surface where the shell is weakest, then chisels and scissors to get at the meat.

At least mussels are easy enough to see if they are about, unlike most of the bivalves, which hide themselves under the sand. And while the others do have a certain freedom of movement — they can reach out to the full extent of their feet and then, contracting violently, roll themselves over the ground — the mussel is anchored securely to the sandy gravel. The mussel's anchor warp (the byssus thread) is made of a sticky substance secreted by a gland in the foot. When you consider that it has to do its job in a variety of temperatures and with alternate wettings and dryings involving both salt and fresh water, the byssus thread is a remarkable substance. The mussel is attached by a cat's cradle of these threads, and as the tidal currents ebb and flow, the shell is free to turn and present the least resistance to the moving sea; but, if by a quirk of the weather, it becomes inundated with fresh coverings of gravel, it has the facility to up-anchor and throw out new lines.

One way and another, the bivalves that make their home in this unlikely sandy environment manage to move as much as they need to. None of them is exactly a fast mover, although scallops, for instance, can leap about in the water by closing their valves together so fast that they are jet-propelled for an appreciable distance – far enough to get away from a hungry starfish. The most spectacular disappearing trick, however, is one performed by the razorshell. The straight smooth shell, often seen lying about on the beach, is beautifully designed to offer least resistance to the sand when the living animal inside decides to pull itself deeper. In the ordinary way, apart from the odd occasion when a storm may uncover it, it will remain out of sight, only a shallow depression at the surface giving a clue to its whereabouts. These depressions are not easy to find, and the best way of discovering the animal is to walk slowly backwards along the wet sand of the lower shore at spring tides. If you do the job properly, then you are rewarded with a sudden squirt of water as you tread near the shell. Dig quickly, and grasp the fast-disappearing shell with the finger and thumb of one hand while you continue revealing it with the other. Like the cockle, it is a suspension feeder, offering short siphons to sample the passing sea water while the tide is in. Its enormous foot, filling about half the shell, is its insurance against predators. Under attack, it heaves itself vertically downwards, very fast indeed.

Many other animals make a good living in the sand, but all of them depend on having learnt a way of digging into it. Without that facility they would be eaten, either by the fish when the tide was in, or by the birds when the tide was out. The regular incursions of tidal water are vital to the well-being of molluscs. Apart from the charge of nutrients and oxygen brought in with every flooding tide, the water content of the sand is important to the animals because it can affect their ease of burrowing. As a lugworm or a cockle forces its way through the sand, it exerts a pressure on the particles which, if there is not much water present, makes the sand harder and more difficult to penetrate. Sands that contain a lot of water react in the opposite way – they become softer and easier to penetrate. These 'thixotropic' sands, of which quicksands are a most unpopular example, are the most attractive to sand burrowing animals and, as the tide rises, bringing in more and more water, conditions in the wet sand gradually become more favourable.

No town council is likely to advertise the desirable qualities of quicksands; they are trying to attract people, not lugworms. Firm sand is all-important to places like Bournemouth, Blackpool, Torquay and Teignmouth. Many of the places which boast fine sands occupy bays, because it is in such sheltered situations that the longshore drift, constantly moving sand along the coast, is slowed down or stopped by any obstacle, like a headland. Sand is such a desirable commodity that sometimes seaside authorities erect artificial barriers, called groynes, to curb the natural drifting of sand. These groynes are vital to resorts which would otherwise have their sand moved on. Their effectiveness can be seen by examining the difference in level between sand on the up- and down-drift side of the groyne.

The part of a groyne that is above the level of the high tides makes a useful lee for sunbathers on a windy day, and a good place for jumping-off games, but the portion extending down into the water also has value for animals and plants. Seaweeds may establish themselves by holding fast to this rare fixed point in a desert of (to them) uninhabitable sand, and around the seaweeds a whole community of animals may find a living, as we shall see when we look at rocky shores. Acorn barnacles and mussels may attach themselves to the wooden surface of a groyne, and chitons may roam about scavenging. Over a long period of time the voracious gribble may eat the timber away. During the course of its useful life, a groyne will accumulate sand, building it higher and higher until the groyne itself is completely buried and the top sand is always above the reach of the sea. The weeds and mussels that made their home on the artificial reef must then look elsewhere for security.

The value placed on sand can be illustrated by the great cost of groyne building. The latest sand traps at Teignmouth, for example, constructed from solid greenheart timber and sunk into the bedrock, cost £1,500 each. The extra sand is ideal for Teignmouth, but this process is of course simply a matter of robbing Peter to pay Paul. The sand which is retained by those baulks of timber will not reach the next sandy beach up the coast. Demand for sand exceeds supply, and the supply is diminishing as more and more coastline is protected by sea walls, promenades, and the sandy beaches themselves. If the sea cannot reach the raw coast to batter and gnaw at the rocks new grains of sand cannot begin their life.

In the face of such diminishing supply some authorities, like Bournemouth, have experimented with artificial seaweed – a series of synthetic fronds anchored offshore in the wave-breaking zone. Unlike groynes, this weapon in the beach-loss armoury is not effective against longshore drift, but instead encourages sandy deposits offshore to move towards the beach.

There is great pleasure in wading through the shallow water at the tide's edge, for on a calm, clear day you will see a great deal of life there. Small hermit crabs scurry about the sea bed. Shrimps and small fish dart and chase. In the summer there

Terns fishing for sand eels

may be terns chattering and calling as they quarter the inshore waters looking for sand eels, picking them daintily off the very surface of the sea, and only barely getting themselves wet. Sand eels, or lance, live at the lowest tide mark, and during the infrequent periods of exposure to the air they lie buried under the sand, using their strong lower jaw as a digging tool. They are much eaten by larger fish, by the terns, and by wading birds like sanderling.

Sanderling are plump little waders with short straight bills. Breeding on the barren Arctic tundra, far from the seashore, they visit coastal Europe in the winter, although non-breeding birds may well be seen during the summer. Once seen they are never forgotten, always seeming to be in a panic, dashing along the water's edge like clockwork toys — hardly having time to stop and eat the sandhoppers and small stuff in the backwash before expertly avoiding the swash.

Weever fish, with its poisonous dorsal spines

The only drawback to wading in the low-water sandflats is the possibility of an encounter with a weever. Half-buried under the sand, this little fish has modified dorsal spines that can inject a powerful poison. While this poison may be ideal for immobilising a passing shrimp, it can be a very unpleasant experience indeed for a human foot. (Treatment is to dip the foot into very hot water.) So shore walking and wading is not without its hazards, but it is a good deal safer than walking along any road.

The most likely danger is that of treading on a piece of glass, and on any popular beach it is probably safe only to walk in shoes. Watch out for nails in timber wreck, too. I once had a nail that went right through a pair of heavy gumboots and into my heel; it was painful for a long time afterwards.

Oil, in liquid form and in the tarry ball version, is a real menace on beaches nowadays, and we must assume that it will be a chronic problem so long as our economy demands continuous injections of oil as an energy source.

On the small scale, eucalyptus oil (from the chemist's shop) will clean your body, your clothes or your carpets with ease, and, incidentally, you can use it safely on a dog's paws. But on the large scale, when a beach is covered in oil, it is not so easy to know what to do. If the oil is in the form of tarry balls, then it can be collected and burned. Burying it actually slows down the rate of disintegration, though it may make it less of a nuisance for the time being. The fact is that if you do nothing and leave the oil where it is, micro-organisms which enjoy eating it will multiply and reduce it over a period of a few months.

If they are properly controlled, dispersants can be sprayed on the oil to break it into small droplets. In the *Torrey Canyon* disaster, as much or more damage was done to intertidal flora and fauna by millions of gallons of toxic dispersant recklessly spread on the beaches, and they took two years or more to recover. At least the affair prompted research, and nowadays dispersants have been produced that have a very low toxicity. It is still necessary to use them correctly, and in the right place, and above all, to make sure they are thoroughly mixed with the oil. Contingency plans are more highly developed, nowadays, so that the inevitable oil spills are, at least in the main, dealt with efficiently.

There is a whole world of horror in the very word 'quicksands', yet the danger is not serious if you deal with the situation calmly. Get to know the local danger spots, if any, and avoid them. Avoid a patch of mud covered with slimy green algae in the midst of clean mud. If by mischance you do start to sink, don't thrash about, but lean gently forward with spread arms, then 'swim' your way back to safety. Keep your body horizontal and spread your weight about.

Stingrays do occur as far north as 51°, so they are a possible danger; the electric ray is not uncommon in the English Channel, and has been taken in waters as far north as Scotland. Rays are beautifully adapted to 'flying' underwater but when they lie on the sea bed they are very difficult to see. They frequent sand and mud bottoms, and have tail stingers that can drive through your foot, leaving a wound liable to infection. The stingray has a serrated poison spine on the back of the tail. The electric ray can give a shock severe enough to knock a fully grown man down if he accidentally steps on it.

So do not walk in too genteel a manner in shallow sandy water at low tide. Poke about ahead of you and shuffle along causing a commotion. That way, weevers and rays and all fierce beasts will know you are coming and prudently go somewhere else.

Jellyfish need watching. The Portuguese man-o'-war has long tentacles that produce painful stings and severe swelling, which may last several hours. The greatest danger is that it may cause a swimmer to panic or get cramp. Difficult though it may be in practice, the correct procedure is to relax. Once ashore, prompt application of ammonia will relieve the pain. Native, but still uncommon, jellyish are *Cyanea capillata*, a gaudy east-coast beast of blue and violet, hung with eight bunches of tentacles, and *Chrysaora isosceles*, which is anything from 4 to 18in (10 to 46cm) across, milk white with a brown central spot and brown radii, found in the south and west. The commonest jellyfish of all, *Aurelia*, with its four purple-violet rings, does have stinging tentacles but they are hardly powerful enough to affect human skins.

Rhizostoma octopus is the largest jellyfish to reach our shores, sometimes in enormous numbers in a warm summer, when they may be seen in seemingly endless shoals. The pale blue or green bell may be as much as two feet across. Though, like *Aurelia*, they pose no danger to us, they are themselves subject to attack by the turtles which may well be in company with them. I once sailed alongside a massive leatherback turtle which was biting into *Rhizostoma* with great gusto and causing the unfortunate jellyfish to spin like a top.

Conger eels can bite and lash you with their tails; octopuses can bite and entwine you with their tentacles, but as they are mostly concerned to give you a wide berth it is unfair to class them as horrors. Congers may be 6ft (1.8m) long and weigh 100lb (45kg), so treat them with respect. An octopus that might be big enough to be dangerous lives in the ocean depths, a very good place for him too.

In case you feel a shark or killer whale might carry you off, it is worth remembering that no one has ever been killed or eaten in British waters by either of these creatures. Some shark anglers have been hurt in the process of 'landing' their catch, but I think perhaps they deserve it, for sharking is a feeble sport.

Any or all of these hazards may spoil your day, but the chances are slim. Ignoring all my own pious advice, I have leapt about on beaches and gone shrimping in shallow water for as many years as I can remember without anything worse than a few minor cuts and sunburn. Even if, one day, a weever gets me, I hope I can staunch the tears and take pleasure in observing the clever way he hides in the sand, spying on the shrimps.

At night, when the beach is deserted and the atmosphere is humid, many creatures emerge to enjoy the safety of the dark. Now is the time to make your way down to the water's edge, especially when there is a particularly low tide. You need a torch, and you need to walk quietly, for the night crawlers and scuttlers are shy. The masked crab spends the day time under the sand, out of the way of predatory fish and gulls. During this time he breathes through a tube formed by long antennae, which have a double row of stiff hairs, allowing water to be drawn down to the gill chambers. His hind legs are equipped with long claws adept at digging and scooping into sand. At night he emerges to explore the lower shore and shallow water areas. Unlike the more conventional crabs, this species does not scuttle 'crabwise' – sideways – and it has a rather endearing way of sitting up and looking interested in life.

Other scavengers show themselves in your torchlight. If there is a piece of dead fish on the sand, look around and under it for the tell-tale humps covering the netted dogwhelk, an active searcher for carrion. They're small, but when their questing siphons sense a suspicion of food, they move along at a surprising speed, just under the surface. One way and another, those acres of bare sand are host to an astonishing range and number of animals.

3

The Strandline

Messing about in boats is certainly one of life's great pleasures, and patrolling the strandline of a wide-open sandy bay is another. The waves that transport sand grains to build the beach also deposit a motley collection of floating junk and treasure. Bits of weed, wood, and all sorts of clues to the profuse life of the sea are cast up by the tide. As the time of high water passes and the water recedes, a strand of debris trails along the golden sand and records the high water mark for all to see. Spring tides will amass the debris high up the beach, while subsequent, lesser, tides leave a sequence of lesser strandlines progressing down the beach like contour lines. Storm tides will wash the slate clean and leave it shining and blank ready for the next message to be drawn.

Exploring these strandlines evokes an excitement akin to that of seeing a trawler catch cascade on to the deck when the

Strandline shells

50

net's cod end is released. The light of day will reveal a string of biological treasures, or maybe, a disappointing array of tatty weed and broken fish boxes. But there is always hope; on a beach walk you might find anything from an empty limpet shell to a crate of oranges.

Most typically the strandline will consist of a pile of seaweed fronds and stipes, torn from a nearby rocky shore by wave action. Look carefully and you will probably see that the weed is colonised by hydroids and nibbled by molluscs. There may be egg cases of whelks, rudely deprived of their chance to deposit their larvae into the plankton. The fresh weed itself, if there is enough of it, may attract local gardeners or farmers, who collect it as a fertiliser. (It is said that four women and one man, aided and abetted by a panniered ass, are able to collect six to eight tons in a six-hour day.) Other creatures beside people are glad to see an influx of weed with all its rich feeding possibilities. Pushed to the very top of the beach by the action of the sea, it slowly rots down to a warm glutinous mass. Underneath it the scavenging sandhoppers find a sympathetic home, emerging at night to crawl or leap about; lift a pile of rotting weed and the air will sing as they rise in clouds. These sand fleas, like the winkles, are well on the way to becoming land animals, with their eggs carried in a brood pouch and their young independent of the plankton stage.

There are fully paid-up land animals that also inhabit the seaweed piles, such as beetles, flesh-flies and small oligochaete worms. Kelp flies feed on the decomposing weed, and may be present in enormous numbers. Their eggs, each with a built-in air bubble to help the embryo fly survive the occasional high-water inundation, are laid in the wrack, and subsequently the emerging larvae help in the process of weed decomposition.

Kelp flies on decomposing weed

With this wealth of insect and crustacean food, it is no surprise that, in walking the tideline, you will find you are not the only beachcomber. Other mammals are not uncommon along the seashore. Apart from you and me, foxes regularly patrol beaches and strandlines looking for carrion and for rabbits, which graze and nibble at the vegetation at the top of the beach. Otters often leave their footprints as proof that they go sea-fishing, but you would be very lucky to see one.

Many passerine land birds come to chase flies and sand fleas and their larvae. Robins and sparrows, pied wagtails and starlings all enjoy rich pickings from the weed, in company with shore-birds like rock pipits, purple sandpipers and turnstones. These shore-birds are remarkably well camouflaged, and since they are also rather confiding, unpanicky creatures,

51

you may almost stumble on top of them before they fly off. Even then they are likely to cover only a small distance before they land again, in a small party perhaps, to work over the debris in search of titbits.

September gales and winter storms blow great quantities of weed ashore. Sometimes, if they are violent enough, they may litter the shore with tellins or cockles. Sea mice, too may be deposited in vast numbers. This slug-shaped creature, up to 4in (10cm) long, is in fact a worm; the largest of the British polychaetes, and it is worth examining carefully for the pleasure of its iridescent green and gold hairy coat, and its bristly toothbrush legs. But the great attraction of strandline walking is the element of surprise. Around the next rocky corner, in the next sandy cove, there just might be a full-blown wreck waiting to be rescued. Indeed the activity of 'beachcombing' was traditionally known as 'wrecking' in the far west of Britain.

Talk about 'wrecking' and most people see a vision of swarthy longshoremen setting up false lights on the top of a cliff in dark and stormy weather, and luring innocent sailor-men to an untimely death on the cruel shore. Never was a reputation so richly undeserved. It is not necessary here to relate how coastal people have risked their lives on untold occasions in order to rescue ships and sailors in distress.

However one may deplore it, the fact is that ships do founder, and their cargoes are very often cast ashore. Wreck of varying kinds finds its way ashore from many different sources, and what law-abiding citizen can restrain his natural curiosity? What more natural than that he should investigate the unexpected windfall? On behalf of the Crown, whose foreshore he jealously and protectively patrols, the honest beachcomber does his duty and reports his findings to the Receiver of Wreck. It is only proper, in defending the good name of wrecking, to make it abundantly clear that the activity involves only what the uninitiated calls beachcombing, no more no less. A dyed-in-the-wool Westcountryman never speaks of going beachcombing, he goes wrecking; and if he's lucky he comes home with some wreck – a few nice pieces of timber and maybe a trawl float, or even a bottle with a message in it. He does not encourage ships to destruction. Neither, in truth, does he very often acquaint the Receiver of Wreck with his discoveries. But then no right-minded Receiver would really want a procession of longshore vagabonds (dictionary definition of a beachcomber) laying choice pieces of gribbled planking and trawl floats on his desk. While it is true that, inside territorial waters,

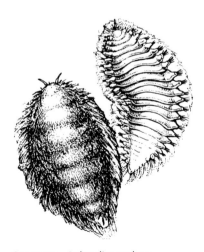

Sea-mouse *Aphrodite aculeata*

52

all wreck is the property of the Crown, it is not too difficult in practice to draw the line between what ought to be reported and what is better quietly tidied away.

Wrecking requires careful preparation. You are not going to wear your Sunday suit or your best shoes. Clearly you will wear old clothes and gumboots or canvas shoes. Remember that if you get them wet with salt-spray, or if you get boots full of sea, they must be washed in fresh water before they will dry properly. For when the sea water dries or evaporates it leaves salt behind, and since the salt is hygroscopic it will always attract moisture from the air. Lovely though it is to walk on the beach with bare feet, and bare everything else for that matter, it is dangerous because of broken glass, not to mention other horrors. You should carry a pocket knife, a couple of yards of Terylene cord for tying bundles of this and that, and a couple of plastic bags for specimens. You should know the times of high and low water and the likely trend of the weather. If you have human competition, then you may have to get up at crack of dawn to be first on the scene.

Some forms of wreck are not so attractive. These are the piles of household rubbish and municipal junk that sometimes get heaved over a cliff to rest in a cove for ages awaiting an extra high tide and storm to wash them away and redistribute them elsewhere. But it can be quite rewarding to search about under jetties and piers or public places where people may have thrown such things as bottles. Ginger beer and pop bottles may date back as far as the middle of the eighteenth century. These are likely to have an almost pointed bottom end, something of a bomb shape. They were eventually patented in 1814 by William Hamilton and were popularly known as Hamiltons, or bowlers, since they were unable to stand up unaided. Later designs introduced a flat bottom and involved a sort of double pinch in the neck, housing a glass marble which, under pressure, sealed the bottle – until it was forced down releasing pressure and allowing the contents to be drunk. Versions of these bottles, and the stone ginger-beer bottles, which usually have a local legend stamped on them, were in common use until the 1940s. Very often you will find that the patent neck has been broken and schoolboys have recycled the glass marble.

You are unlikely to find a pop bottle with its load of pop intact, as they were notoriously unstable and liable to explode, and I suppose the chance of a 'whisky galore' is also slim. But barrels of spirits and wine not infrequently get washed ashore. Mr Williams, the one-time Fisheries Officer at Plymouth, well remembers that during World War II a whole lot of barrels came ashore at Mullion Cove. One was found to contain rum, and this started an avalanche of rescuers combing the beaches. Others contained a very rough red wine. In the 'A hundred years ago' column of the *Western Morning News* a short time ago there was a note about a butt of Tarragona wine which had been washed ashore near Sidmouth in Devon. Nowadays we need to examine all barrels and canisters with a great deal more caution and less happy anticipation because ships' cargoes tend to be more fearful than drinkable. Crude oil is one of the least worrying items when regular cargoes of things like toxic gases and agricultural chemicals trundle up and down the Channel. If you do come across a suspicious canister or war-like object, then you should take careful notes of the inscription and inform the nearest coastguard (see telephone directory).

For wrecking you need a sharp eye. The general technique is obvious enough. Get the light behind you and walk along the strandline, not too fast. Keep your eyes firmly on the strandline, and yet take a long-shot of the distant view occasionally. Especially if there is any opposition, in the form of other wreckers, you must be careful not to miss the big stuff by looking too closely for the small. Sometimes you may have to walk fast slowly to get something someone else is closer to but has not yet seen. But no such technique will find you your basic treasure − coins. On popular beaches there will be favourite places where families spend the day. Invariably and regrettably, some coins fall out of trouser pockets and are lost just under the surface. Gently raking the sand in these places produces quick and substantial results. One almost professional coin collector in Dorset reckoned to make her holiday money in three months using this technique, but she must know her patch very well. On any summer day in St Ives, you may see old men walking slowly across the beach pushing a stick and watching for coins in the furrow.

Succeeding tides may uncover and reveal coins lower down the beach, and if you choose the right place you may be rewarded with gold, or with a genuine Spanish piece-of-eight. One of my friends has some lovely silver coins washed ashore over a period of years from an Armada wreck off the south Devon coast.

But there are other precious objects to be found apart from doubloons. In South Africa they actually find diamonds along the beaches of the south west. Ostriches have the habit of picking up hard stones to use as grinding devices in their gizzards. Naturally enough they prefer diamonds because they offer

Tideline treasure – a piece-of-eight

greatest hardness for a given size. At one time they were in real danger because diamond-hunters would shoot the ostriches in order to examine the gizzard for diamonds. Beach diamond hunting is now a strictly controlled commercial undertaking on a very grand scale. The beach sands are bulldozed and the diamond-bearing gravel screened out and millions of pounds worth of diamonds recovered from this richest deposit in the world.

European coasts cannot compete in the diamond stakes, but there are many semi-precious and ancient things to be found. Coal, for instance, may not have quite the glamour of a diamond, but at least it keeps you warm. Along the shores of the North East, coal waste that has been tipped onto the shore may be collected in hard times by diligent scavengers. In other parts of the country, in the past, poor people have collected the age-old peats and timber from submerged forests, after digging several feet through the sand or by taking advantage of a storm that reveals the ancient fuel. Coal represents the fossilised remains of primitive vegetation from the marsh deltas of hundreds of millions of years ago; diamonds have the same origin.

On the Yorkshire coasts there is a deposit of carbonaceous shale, which yields small lumps of pure coal called jet. A semi-precious material, once highly prized for jewellery, it has been used by craftsmen ever since the Bronze Age. It dates from about 170 million years ago and is the fossilised version of a tree related to the monkey puzzle. Easily carved, it gives off an aromatic odour. Warm to the touch, and a bad conductor of heat, it generates a charge of static electricity when rubbed on fabric.

Perhaps the hey-day of jet jewellery was after the death of Prince Albert, when demand was great and the men of Whitby scoured the beaches after every tide to keep the craftsmen busy. Whitby was the recognised centre for the industry, although jet was found as far away as Kent, carried south by currents.

The raw jet is black only after it has been polished, or broken. The sea-washed pebbles look dull grey and scratchy. The procedure for identifying it is to rub the suspected pebble with emery paper — if brown scratch-lines appear, then it is jet. Nowadays there is no great demand for the material in Britain, although a few Whitby craftsmen remain, but it is still worked on the Continent and in the USA.

Another very beautiful semi-precious stone which may be current-borne to us from the lignite beds of the Baltic, is amber. A fossil resin, some 40 million years old, it comes from the remains of coniferous trees of the Oligocene epoch. The most important amber-producing region is East Prussia, and I well remember the pleasure of finding a piece the size of a pigeon's egg in a shop in Warsaw. It is systematically mined on the coast of Danzig. Like jet it generates static electricity when rubbed against soft cloth, and in fact the Greeks, who first discovered the phenomenon, called it *electron*. Rough amber beads were worn in prehistoric times, and many primitive beliefs attached to them. In Britain amber is found on the shores of the east coast, mostly in Norfolk and Suffolk, where it is nearly always tangled with seaweed and only too easy to miss. Amber comes in two forms, cloudy and an almost clear 'ice colour'. The clouded variety contains water droplets which have dried out, leaving behind their impressions. The clearer version is probably formed by bleaching.

The only connection between amber and ambergris is in the name, for ambergris is a very different substance indeed, with no relation to the fossilised resins and carbons. Sadly, your chance of finding any is very remote, unless you are sailing the China Seas, Indian Ocean or the tropical Atlantic. In fact, the penalties for finding it, and keeping it, can be severe. In the Maldive Islands all ambergris belongs to the Sultan, and you conceal it at risk of decapitation.

Ambergris is a concretion found, rarely, in the intestines of sperm whales, a product which may perhaps be compared with the intestinal stones or hair balls that occur in other smaller whales and in domestic cows. It is a pliable wax-like substance, brown or yellowy-grey; it smells musky and is highly soluble in organic solvents. Lighter than water, it melts at about 149°F (65°C) and dissolves readily in absolute alcohol, ether, fat or vegetable oils. It has been used for centuries as a vehicle to retain and prolong the scent of perfume.

If ambergris is used as a fixative, scents retain their odour for months, so it is not surprising that it has great value, although the market has now passed its peak. In the Orient, it was prized as a powerful aphrodisiac, so its use in the expensive perfumes of today is logical enough.

A piece of ambergris weighing 44lb (20kg) was sold in London for £2,018 in 1924, incidentally turning the Harris Whaling and Fishing Co Ltd's trading account to a profit in what had been a bad year. In 1953 Robert Clarke was on board *Southern Harvester* when a piece of ambergris weighing 918lb (416kg) was removed from the gut of a sperm whale, but even this was surpassed by a vessel of the Dutch East Indies Company which found one weighing 975lb (442kg). No wonder it is every beachcomber's dream to find some, when it is still so valuable. But beware of the many imitations. Paraffin wax, gastropod spawn and decomposed soapstone are all traps for the unwary.

One last word about precious stones. In both the oyster and the ormer there is the slight chance of finding a pearl. In the Channel Islands, where the ormer, a succulent Mediterranean species of limpet is common, I was once shown a small palmful of little pearls that a local fishmonger had painstakingly collected. I hardly imagine that they have much market value, but they were very attractive and made an unusual souvenir.

At one time pearls were thought to contain powerful medicinal properties. Dissolved in lemon juice or mixed with milk they were believed to cure stomach ulcers, improve your speaking voice and preserve chastity.

On the other hand, cowrie shells were more closely connected with conception and birth. With their superficial resemblance to the vulva, they have been much used in the form of amulets, guaranteed to guard against sterility and encourage children. Again, with a resemblance to a human eye, they were worn to give protection against the evil eye. Quite apart from their visual suitability, they lend themselves easily to necklace making, since they are easy to bore and often come ashore with convenient holes broken in them already.

Cowries used to circulate as currency in parts of Africa, and even today the children of the Isles of Scilly call them 'moneypennies'. European cowries are rather small by tropical standards, but have the same shape and attractive characteristics. There are only two species found round our shores, both about half an inch (12mm) long with 20 to 25 ribs. Feeding on sea-squirts, they live under rocks at extreme low water. The European cowrie has three brownish-purple spots and the Arctic cowrie is spotless. Both are common round our shores, although the European is rather more so than the Arctic. In their stranded shell-only form, they are rather difficult to find, being well camouflaged among the beach debris. But on a suitable beach, like that on Tresco in Scilly, or Bantham in Devon, you may find a good number. As an exercise, once, I spent twenty minutes concentrating on the job, and found 61 on the shell beach at Bantham; 35 were European and 26 Arctic cowries.

Cowrie shells bring a breath of the tropics to our beaches. Better (since they at least are honest citizens of Britain), than the dismal trade in tropical cowries and murex and cone shells that fill seaside souvenir shops in the summer. Fantastic shapes and beautiful colours they may have, but the trade is vile; the unfortunate inhabitant of the shell is boiled out just to provide a cheap and inappropriate souvenir.

I know that, to a serious collector, the only shell worth talking about is the perfect one that has been taken off the back of its live owner, but for most of us I like to think that the slightly battered and sun-bleached version thrown up on the beach is just as interesting. Often the 'lantern' – a helical whorl – is all that is left of a whelk shell on the strandline, and a very intriguing and shapely thing it is, too. Often a shell will bear the signs of the animal that killed its occupant. A neatly bored round hole indicates that the carnivorous dog whelk has done his dirty work. And there may be the tube cases of bristle worms, limy scribblings and spiralling. One shell may have other shells and acorn barnacles clinging to it, forming a block of flats, and in rock pools it may have been taken over by a new inmate, the hermit crab.

Beach pebbles are worth examining closely, since they come in such a variety of colours and shapes. Few people can resist collecting the more attracive ones, but it is not so easy to know how to make use of them (apart from the pleasure of chucking them into the sea, one of the least harmful ways known to man of sublimating his aggressive instincts on difficult days). You can invest in a 'tumble polisher', which, over a period of time, transforms the rough pebble surface into a gem. Mount it, thread a length of leather thong, and . . . instant hippy. There is quite a thriving business in this sort of thing in the Westcountry; Kernowcraft of Bolingey, Perranporth, Cornwall, have an excellent catalogue if it interests you.

Sand-polished pieces of glass floats, pop and wine bottles, can look very attractive if they are piled into an old decanter or flagon, covered with water and placed on a windowsill where the sun may shine through them. One of those old-fashioned goldfish bowls would be ideal for the job, especially as they are highly unsuitable for keeping goldfish.

Timber, in varying shapes and sizes, from fish boxes to ships' hatch covers, is one of the most useful things to be salvaged from the beach. It is the staple diet of a wrecker's day. I wonder how many old coastal cottages and houses did not have some beach timber built in somewhere. In the Isles of Scilly, every self-respecting farmer-fisherman has a wreck pile from which he selects the required piece of wood for the job in hand.

Much of it is softwood, and very often irretrievably damaged by marine borers and fit only for the fire, but often enough you may find a nice piece of iroko or oak on the beach. Perhaps a portion of deck cargo that has been washed away; when it is rain washed and dried out there is a lifetime of use in it.

Not only cut timber, but the trees themselves may end up on the tide line. Torn by the roots in time of flood or avalanche, they are riverborne and finally seaborne. They may even carry large rocks in their roots so that eventually the rock is left, out of its geological context, to puzzle and intrigue. In studying Arctic sea currents, it was found that stranded trees could be traced back to their home valleys. Different climates and different valleys produced a recognisable variation in the character of the tree rings so that a study of trees cut down *in situ* made it possible to identify the origin of tree trunks stranded a great distance away from home.

After heavy rains, great islands of floating reed mats may form in estuaries. They carry with them a rich assortment of vegetation and a floating oasis of unwilling animal voyagers. Tens of miles off the mouth of the River Congo, a young negro was once discovered sitting on a floating tree island of this sort. These mobile tropical islands are not infrequent and, sometimes massive enough to be a danger to shipping, are the subject of special 'Notices to Mariners'. One of the theories relating to the remote Pacific Galapagos Islands is that its unique flora and fauna was enriched over a long period by animals which arrived on vegetable islands formed in the Ecuadorian deltas, 600 miles (965km) away.

Nearer Britain, it is by no means unusual to see small mounds of debris floating downhill on our own estuaries, and it is reasonable to assume that they carry unwilling insect passengers. Often you see a pied or grey wagtail, or a gull, taking a ride and investigating the possibilities.

Tree roots often assume most intriguing shapes after they have been scoured by sea and sand. Mostly they have a serpentine appearance and many people have driftwood snakes on their mantlepieces. Others use a driftwood tree, scoured and sculptural, as a garden bird-table support.

Pit props are fairly common beach finds. Short cut sections of spruce, they often get washed overboard on passage as deck cargo from Scandinavian ports to South Wales. Early in February 1961, in a storm, for safety's sake a coaster deliberately cut adrift some 60,000 pit props that were travelling as deck cargo. They came ashore on the north Cornish coast, which soon became a scene of intense activity. Many people were collecting the timber for firewood, but farmers, who have an infinite variety of uses for wreck, brought tractors and trailers in order to make greatest use of the windfall. One of the collectors was so enthusiastic he waded into the sea to reach the floating pit props. A big wave swept him off his feet and out to sea to a watery grave.

In dirty weather, an unprepared ship will lose a variety of gear from her deck. Hatch covers were, not so long ago, a fairly common and most useful discovery on the beach, but nowadays they are almost always made of slatted steel, which has much greater strength and resistance to the grasping sea, so they remain firmly attached to the deck.

Again, after bad weather, it may happen that cargo from some long-sunk wreck may break out and litter a beach for miles. There is nothing quite so exciting as the sight of a stretch of beach spread with an assortment of broken and unbroken boxes and general chaos. Canned fruit, raisins, tobacco, wine casks, marine oil, tallow – the possibilities are endless, even if reality is not always quite so rewarding. A life-long wrecker once wrote to tell me of one such morning: '. . . . just after the war there was some tobacco which came up in cases from a Yankee liberty ship which broke off here. I went early one morning with my nephew at first light, and stretched across the beach was case after case. We rushed down. I gave the first one a kick and heard tins rattling inside. I thought to myself, "Corn in Egypt", which is a local saying if we thought we had struck it lucky. Took the lid off and they were filled with pine tins of Emergency Drinking Water, tinned in America, so that was a let down! We buried some in the dunes and used to tap them if we were thirsty.' This same man tells of many bales of rubber which may have come from a ship originally sunk in World War I. They weighed 100lb (160kg) each, and although he got £5 each for them he reckoned he had earned it by the time he got them off the beach and up the cliff. He believes that quite a lot of people make a good living from wrecking.

However, there is a whole world of interest in a length of

timber that is not worth a penny piece. Examine the tatty and long-travelled pieces of wood on the shore and you will very often find that they have been carrying passengers which were not at all pleased to reach land. (Incidentally, an oceangoing fish, commonly found sheltering underneath drifting timber, bears the highly suitable name of wreckfish.) During its time at sea the surface of floating wood may have been colonised by creatures which, floating about in the plankton, were looking for a more permanent home. Acorn barnacles and goose barnacles are most likely to be found on the outside surfaces. The goose barnacles, curious creatures with a striking likeness to the head and neck of a bird, are stalked barnacles that have cemented themselves to the timber during its time in warmer parts of the Atlantic. In the days of slow-moving ships they attached themselves in numbers underneath the waterline and then grew fat, doing no good to the vessel's hydrodynamic shape and much reducing her speed.

Like the more conventional acorn barnacles ashore, the goose barnacle opens protective plates to reveal feathery *cirri*, which filter food from the passing plankton. Originating from warmer parts of the Atlantic, these beautiful creatures are usually destined to die on our beaches, but you might find some, attached to a small piece of wood or even a bottle, which might respond, at least temporarily, to immersion in a tank of sea water. If you are lucky, they will emerge in all their feathery glory, to feed.

It was because of their feathery appearance, and the curiously beak-shaped protective plates on the neck-like stalks, that goose barnacles got their name. For many hundreds of years it was popularly believed that these barnacles were the juvenile form of the barnacle goose, and it is not at all difficult to sympathise with the misunderstanding. Often enough the barnacles are washed ashore attached to floating tree branches. So the myth took shape: 'Certain of their trees bear fruit which, decaying within, produces a worm which, as it subsequently develops, becomes hairy and feathered, and, provided with wings, flies like a bird'.

Doubtless the educated medieval mind was well aware of the faults in this argument, but there was a powerful incentive to allow it to prevail. With such a clearly maritime origin, the barnacle goose could comfortably be classified as a fish, and as such its meat could be eaten on Fridays and feast days. It was not until 1187 that Gerald the Welshman reproved the laxity of Irish priests, and soon afterwards Innocent III forbade the practice by decree. It was the middle of the seventeenth century before a Jesuit had the temerity to declare that, although no one knew where the goose was born (in fact in Greenland, Spitzbergen and Novya Zemlya), it nevertheless was hatched from an egg, incubated like any other goose. For all that, the earlier myth was happily kept in circulation for the convenience of gourmet clerics.

Barnacles congregate on the outside of drifting timber, but there are other creatures active inside. They are of special interest to mariners because they can cause a great deal of damage and indeed, in severe cases, they may cause a ship to founder. Since the earliest days of civilisation ships have suffered from the attacks of 'worm'. Fouling by barnacles and seaweed reduced the speed of a ship and was dealt with by regular careening and scraping, but until the sheathing of underwater hulls with copper no one could counter the destructive marine borers. It was found that the interaction of sea water with the copper produced a slow release of copper salt solution which was toxic to the ship worm. Copper is expensive, so today the work of discouraging attack by marine borers is done by anti-fouling paints that still use the same principle of slowly releasing a toxic copper salt solution.

The pieces of wood thrown up on the beach are unlikely to have been protected by anti-fouling paint, and are very often extensively damaged by the most common of the borers, ship worm and gribble. The gribble, despite its rather attractive name, is a voracious beast, a crustacean isoped looking much like a miniature beach sand-hopper. It attacks wood from the surface, making minute holes about $1/5$in (5mm) diameter and then excavating shallow galleries about $1/10$in (2.5mm) deep. Because it is so numerous the galleries soon merge together, the surface of the timber is destroyed, and the timber gets wetter and softer. Jetty and pier piling subjected to this kind of attack may eventually collapse altogether.

The crustacean gribble

The shipworm is a mollusc with powerful boring valves

The shipworm – *Teredo* – is not a worm at all, but a particularly destructive bivalve mollusc. It certainly looks like a worm, and may be as much as 1ft (30cm) long, but at the end of its body is its shell, greatly reduced in size and a highly specialised boring device. It penetrates timber in its larval stage, making a very small entrance hole. Once inside it takes a smart right-angle turn and then digs out a tunnel lengthways just inside the surface, so that although you cannot see it, it is literally eating the plank, or whatever, away. The teredo cuts its tunnel as it grows, burrowing with a twisting movement of the shell. There are three species in British waters, the largest, *Teredo norvegicus*, is also the commonest. It is rather more common in the south than in the north, and is most active from April through to October. In the tropics some species grow up to 5ft – 1.5m – long, a horrid thought for any boat owner.

The gribble effect is easy to spot, but teredo may only be revealed by splitting the timber open, although the presence of many small, round, cleanly cut holes is a clue. The result of splitting a well eaten log is quite spectacular. If the wood is newly cast ashore it is more likely that you will see the complete worm, but if it has been out of the sea for some time you will have to look carefully to see the remains of the creature – just the cutting edges, the two shells. Teredo attacks wooden pier piling too, and it is an animal to be taken very seriously.

Small boats, at least, are nowadays mostly made of glass reinforced plastics, and this is one way of reducing the likelihood of damage by gribble and teredo. Teredo has been known to attack plastics, so it may be that in the long run it will even learn to deal with the new breed of yachtsmen, but there is no doubt that beaches are going to be less rewarding places for wreckers as the GRP revolution continues. An old wooden ship gently rotting on a beach provides a quantity of interest, both in natural phenomena and from the pleasure of seeing the harmonious construction of keel, frames and planking. But we must adapt to change and learn to enjoy the plastic artefacts that decorate the tideline, detergent bottles and flip-flop shoes, which may have come from far-off places, and stretch our command of language to read their inscriptions. Sometimes they too will have bristle worms and barnacles attached to them, and jammed in the right place they may provide a home for a crab or an anemone.

Perhaps the strangest innovation is plastic seaweed, which I suppose in due course may also become a common strandline object after storms, like its natural progenitor. The original idea is said to have come from a Danish fisherman, who noticed the way seaweed has a calming effect on the sea. Developed in order to combat coastal erosion, loss of sand in particular, the weed is made of 8ft (2.5m) lengths of polypropylene tape, looking somewhat like thongweed. Tufts of the tape are attached at one yard (or one metre) intervals to lengths of steel chain,and then laid in rows at right-angles to the shore. The experiment has been tried in the USA and in Holland and Britain (in Yorkshire, Suffolk and Hampshire). Preliminary tests in the sheltered Danish waters resulted in a 39in (1m) build-up of sand over a period of 18 months. Apart from the obvious value to seaside holiday resorts, it may be that plastic seaweed will prevent erosion and undermining around deep-water

Tropical beans: *Mucuna urens* (top) and *Entada gigas*

pipelines, possibly protect experimental fish breeding grounds and help with the delicate operation of encouraging oyster spat to anchor themselves. However the most difficult problem is apparently to anchor the 'seaweed' itself successfully.

It is difficult to imagine anything more exotic than plastic seaweed on a beach, yet tropical beans are strong contenders. There are two species which arrive on western coasts not infrequently, and they come here after a long Atlantic journey that starts in the Caribbean. A glance at the surface current chart shows the route. Both species are hard and tough objects, but I imagine they would need both those qualities to make such a long passage without being eaten or otherwise attacked. Both are about the size of a large broad bean; one of them, *Entada gigas*, is the same shape. It is a seed which comes from the West Indies, has a uniform brown colour and a hard shiny skin. The other, *Mucuna urens*, shaped more like a disc, has a black creamy bordered rim on a dark purple-brown background. It probably comes from Central America. John Barrett, the marine biologist, says that in his home county of Pembrokeshire parents give the Caribbean bean to babies for them to cut their teeth on.

On the western coast of Ireland and in the Western Isles of Scotland these beans used to be known as 'Marybeans', after the Virgin Mary, because they were thought to bring the owner good fortune. Midwives gave them to women in labour, both as a lucky charm and as a distraction, rather like worry beads.

Dr Charles Nelson, National Botanic Gardens, Glasnevin, Dublin 9, is collecting information on these vegetable immigrants and where they land, so he would be delighted if you send him any strange seeds or beans you find washed up on the beach. He needs to see the bean itself because some species are very hard to identify from description alone. He would like to know where and when you found it, and also your name and address so that he can return your lucky charm.

Sometimes deep sea jellyfish are stranded on our beaches in large numbers. This happens, mainly on western coasts, after a long period in which south-west winds have persistently blown them towards us. Both the species stranded this way are by-the-wind sailing creatures, unable to govern their own movements in the way used by the common jellyfish, which swims by opening and closing its discs, thereby producing a sort of slow motion jet propulsion.

The first is called the 'by-the-wind sailor' and is somewhat like our own jellyfish but more oval and with a hard ridge 'sail', which extends right across a diameter. Deep blue round the edge, it is 4in (10cm) or so across. The second is the Portuguese man-o'-war, which is a most wonderfully constructed creature. The bladder, which is the part you are most likely to find on the beach, is up to about 6in (15cm) long, and looks very much like some kind of child's balloon. Indeed it can be difficult to persuade someone that it is animal and not man-made. The float is a pale blue, and there is a crenellated crest of a pinkish colour. From the float hangs a complicated cluster of stinging cells in long tentacles. If the jellyfish is alive, do not touch it as it can deliver a powerful sting. This is its method of capturing prey — small fish — in the ocean. Often the animal is somewhat battered by the time it reaches our shores, and the bladder is the only part left. When they do appear, it may well be in very large numbers over a long stretch of coastline.

Home grown jellyfish are frequently stranded. *Aurelia* is the commonest, usually 6 to 8in (15 to 20cm) across, with its four purple rings. A larger, and stinging, animal is *Chrysaora*, milky-white with a central brown spot and radial brown streaks. Then there is *Rhizostoma*, the biggest, up to 2ft (60cm) across and quite harmless; it is pale green or blue with a darker purple fringe.

The egg masses of cuttlefish may sometimes be found on the shore as bunches of small 'grapes'. They may be separated from or still attached to their seaweed anchorage. The adult cuttlefish lives amongst the shallow-water eel grass forests on sandy bottoms, hunting shrimps which it gathers with fast-flung sucker tentacles. Rather surprisingly, the cuttlefish is a mollusc, though certainly a complex form, and its shell — the 'bone' — is one of the commonest strandline finds. In the live animal this cuttlefish 'bone' is a hydrostatic organ that acts as a gas tank with a partial vacuum facility making it possible for the animal to pump water in and out of the buoyancy tank in order to adjust for pressure changes according to operating depths, in more or less the same way as a submarine. A carnivorous beast, the cuttlefish is a complex mollusc related to squid and octopus. Unlike the more familiar snails, which carry their shells on the backs, cuttlefish are actually built around their shells. And it is these shells that end up on the strandline. The living creature has five pairs of tentacles with suckers, which it uses for seizing prey. Leslie Jackman, who runs the aquarium by Paignton Harbour, once had a cuttlefish which would take prawns from his hand, rather like a robin coming for mealworms. It would approach slowly, changing colour as it moved and betraying its emotion, jet propelling itself by forcing water through a funnel formed by its foot, then suddenly seize the

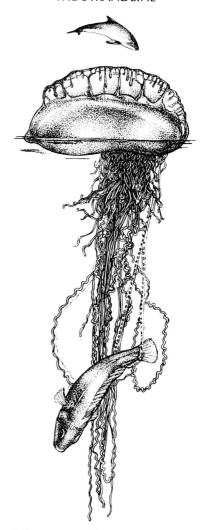

Portuguese man-o'-war

The grape-like egg mass of the cuttlefish, attached to seaweed

65

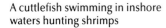
A cuttlefish swimming in inshore waters hunting shrimps

prey and deliver it to the parroty beak of its mouth. Striped almost in zebra fashion, the common cuttlefish may be up to 12in (30cm) long. The other species are smaller, round about the 2 to 5in (5 to 12.5cm) mark. They are widely distributed and common, especially on southern coasts. The scientific name *Sepia* describes the dark brown fluid taken from a small sac inside the animal, which was used as ink by the Greeks and Romans.

Cuttle-bone is well known to all cage-bird fanciers. Most comes from Portugal, where the flesh of the cuttlefish is brought by housewives and the bone exported to Britain, after being dried on special racks in the sun or treated with infra-red heat. Some was imported from France, and at one time annual imports were of the order of 100 tons – a figure almost as surprising as the belief that budgerigars are now the most-kept pet in England.

If you think of giving a beach-found cuttle-bone to your budgie, bear in mind that, according to the experts, no superior fancier would dream of it. The dirt and grit embedded in the beach specimen might encourage disease. All the same, beach cuttle-bones very often, to the naked eye at least, seem the very essence of purity, and it seems you may give it to your cage bird after you have washed it well, boiled it and dried it thoroughly. If you have a lot of cuttle-bones on your beach and think you might make a fortune by selling to one of the big cage-bird suppliers then I wish you luck, and tell you that the smallest quantity that will interest them is half a tonne.

There are other sea-washed and sun-dried shells to be found on the beach, and how curious that there is nothing macabre about them; they are so perfect and clean that instead of the sort of reaction one half expects in touching mortal remains there is a pleasure in the delicate colouring and structure. Even the empty shell of a spiny spider crab, a harmless beast that gives plenty of people the creepy-crawlies while it is alive, is a pleasure to examine. If it is freshly ashore then it may still have anemones, sea squirts, sponges and barnacles growing in among the prickles of its back. Then there is the red case of the edible crab and the green one of the shore crab. If they are still in the stage of internal decomposition then they will be providing food for strandline scavengers like turnstones and sandhoppers.

Mermaid's purses are one of the more romantic things to find. The horny egg-cases of dogfish, skates and rays, they are usually empty by the time they find their way on to the beach, and a tell-tale slit in the capsule betrays the door through which the young fish launched itself into the sea. Dogfish eggs have an off-white milky colour, and are easily identified by the long curly tendrils that extend from each of the four corners, possibly still lashed to a bit of the weed which formed an anchorage during incubation. The black purses of skates and rays have stiffer, shorter processes at the corners, since they were attached to stones or weed by a sticky part of the main capsule. As in the dogfish, though, the 'horns' have an important function, since they are hollow and allow a current of water to pass to the interior of the capsule, carrying oxygen to the embryo. Sometimes there will be a disaster and the egg breaks free too soon, and the unfortunate remains of the embryo will still be inside the leathery egg case when you find it.

The spongy-yellow egg masses of the common whelk are common on beaches. Varying in size from a golf ball to a football, they too are usually empty and the juvenile whelks have gone before the egg capsules reach the beach, having been torn from their rock anchorages by turbulence. But there may be a certain amount of yolk left, so open them gently (because you may find they squirt liquid at you; sailors and longshoremen have been known to use them instead of soap) and there may well be castaways like long-clawed porcelain crabs hiding inside. These are about the size of your little finger nail, but they have broad prize-fighters' arms. Normally they are found in kelp holdfasts, but it seems that whelk egg-masses have an attraction for them. I once examined fifty of the masses on a beach and found that all but six had the little crabs inside, many of them still alive.

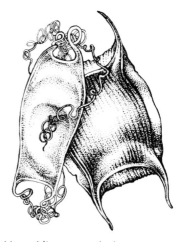

Mermaid's purses – the horny egg-cases of dogfish and skate

67

Over a period of time a great quantity of dead and decomposing animal and vegetable matter gets thrown ashore on beaches, but the scavengers are well able to deal with it. Gulls and turnstones do their bit, but the master cleaners are the great armies of sandhoppers which live in the sand and decaying seaweed during the day, and leap about in the search for food at night. Their many legs are made for jumping as well as for walking (they are called beach fleas in America) and they are to be seen in clouds sometimes, as they make their way down to the fertile lower parts of the beach at low water. They are powerful feeders. I left a pair of woollen bathing trunks on the beach by mistake one night. Next morning they were a ragged mass of holes.

Pieces of string full of holes are most likely to be torn pieces of fishing net. Nowadays they are made from synthetic twines, and highly coloured in orange or blue. They will be from trawl or seine or trammel nets, or possibly even from crab pots, and will be of varying sizes. There are strict laws governing the mesh used to catch fish. For instance in Britain there is an absolute ban on mesh sizes between 2 and 3in (50 and 70mm). Below 2in (50mm) the nets are for pelagic – open water – fish and for shrimps and sprats; above 3in (70mm) for demersal – bottom feeding – fish. But you are likely to find almost any size on the beach. Unfortunately, the better quality synthetic lines such as nylon and Terylene, which would be a welcome find, have a high specific gravity and sink to be lost for ever, whereas the cheaper and less useful polythene and polypropylene versions float for ever, sometimes to wrap themselves around boat propellers or to be carried off to line sea-bird nests, with dire results. Nylon fishing line of the type used by anglers comes ashore in dangerous little balls, usually wrapped in a bundle of seaweed which has torn adrift, providing buoyancy.

Plaited polythene is used a great deal by deep-sea trawlers, and to some extent in small trawls and gill nets. Synthetic line comes in a bewildering number of forms, and with an equally bewildering number of functions, but polypropylene twines tend to be of a natural colour, or green or brown, and polythene comes plaited or twisted and orange in colour. These are the ones most likely to be found on the beach. Black polythene is used for crab pot netting because it is less susceptible to damage by the ultra-violet rays of direct sunlight when the pots are out of the water. It is the main disadvantage of synthetic lines that, if left in hot sun, they may deteriorate to a condition where they will collapse without warning. But, on the other side of the coin, they are strong, weather-resistant and less liable to swell up in the wet than natural fibre ropes.

The iron, glass and plastic floats used by fishermen are one of the commonest beach finds. I once had a collie bitch whose greatest delight was to see one while it was still drifting; she would swim out and turn it over and over until she got a grip on the lug, and then bring it ashore to play football and bark. Often when you find them on the shore the lug is broken but this is less likely with the incredibly tough new plastic version.

The various kinds of floats are used to hold fishing nets upright in the water and they are counterbalanced by lead or chain sinkers which pull the nets downward to the sea bed. Many floats come from trawls – enormous bags of netting with a great mouth perhaps 80ft (25m) across. The lower lip, a weighted foot rope, sweeps the bottom, the mouth held open by otter boards which sheer out like submarine kites as the apparatus is towed along. The upper-lip, or headrope, is kept up with a row of floats. These may have to withstand enormous pressure, and that is one reason for their invariable ball shape. Seiners and some trawlers fish in depths of up to 60 fathoms (110m); their floats are anything from 5 to 10in (12.5 to 25cm) in diameter with a single welded lug. In Arctic waters trawlers may be working as deep as 300 fathoms (550m) so it is clear that the trawl floats, although much the same size as the shallow water versions, have to be strong. These floats always used to be made of galvanised iron or aluminium and, since there are large numbers in circulation this kind is likely to be coming ashore for a long while yet. Some of them have one or more metal rims around the outside. These are specially designed to impart an upwards planing movement when the trawl is being towed forwards. Some steel floats are painted but the aluminium ones are always the natural grey colour, and have the advantage that they do not corrode. Buoyancies range from about 2lb (.9kg) for a 5in (12.5cm) diameter steel float to about 14lb (6kg) for a 10in (25cm) aluminium alloy one.

There was some doubt about the suitability of plastic floats when they first appeared, and salesmen had to be convinced of their value. At the headquarters of the famous Bridport Gundry works in Dorset, a group of representatives was taken to the Board Room and shown the new toys. These were a hollow plastic float made in one piece of a very hard, impact-resisting plastic, coloured white or light orange, with buoyancies of up to 9lb (4kg) and a maximum working depth of 500 fathoms (900m). The salesmen were not too impressed, and were invited to throw them out of the first floor window onto an asphalt drive below. After an afternoon's efforts, during which time little other work got done, they only managed to break one float. The galvanised version was doomed. Bridport Gundry claim that their 'permolift supa' trawl floats have a distinctive orange colour, which is ideal for night fishing under arc lamps, and that in daylight the colour appears neutral to fish.

The floats originate from almost any European country, mainly from Norway, but some come from as far as the Far East, and the embossed designs can be very attractive. They include the maker's name and country of origin, and sometimes they bear a figure indicating tested working depth, for instance 'prof 800m'. Seine nets may be floated by dozens of cork 'doughnuts' or by as many as thirty of the well known glass floats — fortune-teller's globes of green, brown, or blue translucence. But these too have been superseded by ball or egg-shaped plastic floats, and the corks by similarly shaped PVC or polystyrene. Some fishermen like to use the cork floats still because, after a lifetime of experience, they know exactly how many to use to get the kind of buoyancy they need. But there is not much doubt that there will be fewer and fewer corks and glass balls in use and inevitably fewer coming ashore. The expanded PVC or polystyrene floats, whether of solid or hollow construction, are almost ideal for the job, being impervious to water and highly resistant to weathering. They are made in a wide variety of colours, which certainly adds something to the wrecking scene.

Floats of solid construction are mainly from Norway, while Denmark was the first country to introduce the hollow plastic version; grey coloured spheres from 3 to 8in (7.5 to 20cm) in diameter, with grooved holes instead of lugs for attaching to the head line.

This grooved type is now also made in Britain, white or grey for deep-water trawls and orange for use on seine nets in depths up to about 100 fathoms (180m). Then again there is a very commonly used Norwegian soft PVC material buoy, orange coloured and ball shaped, with a single moulded lug. This is designed for use in shallow water. For the same purpose there are expanded polystyrene solid floats of a mottled blue-grey colour, made in Norway for use on surface floatlines. These solid floats come in a bewildering variety of sizes and shapes — egg, ball, cylinder — and with a variety of holes and grooves. Mostly they are small by comparison with the trawl floats.

Like the galvanised trawl floats, the glass balls inevitably less common on beaches, and will perhaps become collector's pieces. One of the pleasures of early morning wrecking used to be the colourful glistenings of a glass float in the wet sand and the low sun. It is true that you can buy a bowdlerised version in souvenir shops, but these are of inferior and fragile construction, and the string netting that encloses them is a poor thing compared with the kind made of codline by a fisherman. Not surprisingly perhaps, the souvenir shop float costs rather more than the commercial variety.

Dan buoys, sometimes known as dhan, or danh, are the marker buoys, often with a flag on top, which mark the end position of set nets or longlines. They may be Heath Robinson affairs made of a few cork doughnuts threaded and lashed to a stick, or they may be of cylindrical polystyrene, or spherical or pear shaped. The most expensive ones are made of inflated PVC. They are very tough and weather resistant and are brightly coloured to make them easy to locate from a distance. They may be anything from 40 to more than 100in (100 to 250cm) in circumference. The same inflated PVC technique is used for a number of other types of marker and mooring buoys and some of them used as fenders. In fact, you need to bear in mind that, while manufacturers may well make floats for a specific purpose, they will undoubtedly be used in practice for any number of different jobs. A distant-waters' trawler float constructed to withstand sea pressure at 400 fathoms (730m) may end life after many vicissitudes as a surface marker, connected by a piece of strandline polythene to a crab pot in 5 fathoms (9m) of water. Fishermen are master wreckers!

Modern dan buoys should bear a sequence of letters and numbers which represent the fishing boat's registration mark. Returned to the Receiver of Wreck they attract a reward. Because of the greatly increased activity of coastal shipping, new legislation will enforce fishing vessels to mark their gear more conscientiously. Better and more conspicuous marking of longlines, trammels and crab pots would certainly be popular with anyone who has to make coastal passages in boats. At the moment it is like trying to thread an inshore maze, there are so many poorly marked and dangerous floating lines on the sea.

Cork or plastic lifebuoys and life rafts are exciting discoveries. If the name of the ship and the port of registry is legible then you should report them immediately to the nearest coastguard in case they represent news of value. Mostly they have been lost overboard in undramatic circumstances but you can never be sure until you have checked.

One of the less attractive habits of ships' masters, naval and commercial alike, is that of jettisoning 'gash' at sea. Sooner or later a lot of it finds its way ashore to litter the beaches. On her way home to Portsmouth for paying-off, one well known naval vessel dumped a quantity of unwanted material overboard. The north-west gale that was blowing at the time carried masses of papers to the island of Alderney, where the fields were soon spread with them. The States of Alderney had to get the Public Works Department to round them up for incineration, but confirmed wreckers now have their own complete copies of useless, but intriguing, Standing Orders.

Sailors seem to make a habit of throwing electric light bulbs away, and in spite of their delicate nature they often end up on the strandline intact. As an exercise, I brought three of them home the other day and tried them in a mains socket. Incredibly, two of them worked, albeit with some ominous fizzing.

A certain amount of food is thrown overboard or lost from ships, and not all of it is recycled by the gulls before it reaches the shore. An extraordinary coincidence in this connection was told to me by Mrs Barbara Benton of the Channel Island of Alderney. Early in 1972 two half-pint cartons of milk, still full, sailed in and landed on an Alderney beach. They were labelled 'Alderney Puritan Milk' yet were packed in Chicago. The curious part of the story is that since the last war there have been, alas, no Alderney cows (a breed in the same sense that Jersey and Guernsey cattle are separate) on the island, and that they exist only in America, where shipments were sent in 1890 and 1910. A strange coincidence that Alderney milk should find its way back home, presumably lost overboard from a ship in the Channel. Milk is an unlikely sort of thing to find on a beach, but on hot days I have eaten, with relish, grapefruit and oranges from the strandline. I draw the line at the extraordinary number of onions sometimes seen, and wait with eternal hope for the traditional barrel of rum.

Fish sometimes turn up dead on the beach, though I think it would be a brave man who ate them, because the flesh deteriorates very fast indeed. It is well worth looking to see whether they carry a metal or plastic number tag — evidence that they are part of a scientific investigation. In Britain the operational headquarters is the Fisheries Laboratory in Lowestoft. The work is planned and co-ordinated by the Ministry of Agriculture Fisheries and Food, using research vessels and sometimes chartered commercial vessels. Fish marking experiments are being carried out in all the major fisheries extending from Spitzbergen to the Irish Sea and Western Approaches. In addition to herring, five of the commoner bottom fish are marked on a large scale – cod, haddock, whiting, plaice and sole. The object of the exercise is to discover the effect of fishing on fish populations, that is to discover what proportion of fish stock is being caught. Long term management, whether by mesh regulation or by closure of certain grounds or other controls, depends on knowledge of this kind.

Naturally, the great proportion of fish tag recoveries is by fishermen themselves, but not infrequently the tags end up ashore. A Russian tag, No 27082, was placed on a cod which was released off Labrador in 1963; it was eventually recovered by a small boy on Torcross beach in Devon in 1969. In more local fish-marking experiments tags often are found by beachcombers.

There are various types of mark, disc, hook or tag, and various materials used; metal, celluloid or plastic. Experiments have shown that different species of fish each have a tag and tag position which suits them best. In the case of plastic flags, the material is impregnated with an anti-fouling compound to inhibit marine organisms from attachment. The treatment is necessary because in British waters the tags were sometimes recovered with 6in (15cm) of weed attached, a somewhat unfair load for a fish to drag around.

Crabs and scallops have also been the subject of marking experiments, although in the case of crabs a difficulty arises when the tag is cast off with the periodic moult. Shellfish or fish tags, if possible complete with owner, should be delivered to the nearest Fishery Office or to the Fisheries Laboratory, Lowestoft, giving date and position of recovery and any other relevant information.

Bird rings may be found on the shore so, if ever you see a dead bird, check its legs. And, sadly, dead birds are only too common around our coasts nowadays. Guillemots and razor-bills are the most likely if there has been an oil spillage, but at one time or another you will see most of the seabirds on the British List, dead from a variety of causes – rough weather, food shortages, chemicals and unknown factors. Auks are the most seriously affected by oil because they have the unfortunate habit of spending a lot of their migration time on the surface of the sea when they are on passage to and from the breeding cliffs and wintering quarters around the Iberian Peninsula and the open Atlantic. They are gregarious birds, they paddle about and socialise, and if they are unlucky they swim into oil patches. The oil gets their feathers in a mess; they preen, and once oil is in their lungs they are very likely doomed. Eventually the sad black-and-white corpse comes ashore. Only a small proportion of ringed birds is recovered, so every recovery is of real value. Send the ring, flattened and stuck to your letter containing information about species, place and date, to the British Trust for Ornithology, Beech Grove, Tring, Hertfordshire.

Both grey and common seals have been ringed or tagged for some years now and, as for dead birds, it is always important to check a seal body in case it is tagged. In the early days we used a monel metal ring, somewhat similar to a bird ring, and clipped it over the 'thumb' of either of the hind flippers. But now there is a much more efficient method that uses cattle tags attached to the seal's tail.

If you do find a dead seal, whether ringed or not, you should report the discovery, including details of place, date, species, sex and age of the animal (if you can manage it!) to the Seals Research Unit, c/o Fisheries Laboratory, Lowestoft, Suffolk.

Several species of turtle, which ought by rights to be confined to the tropical regions, find themselves in British waters, having strayed off-course during their seasonal migrations from breeding beaches to feeding grounds. Once carried off, and current-borne to our temperate zone, they have effectively committed suicide, for they cannot live long in our waters. If you do find one, it is important to inform the nearest Receiver of Wreck (at the local Custom House) or the Coastguard or the Natural History Museum. Your chance of finding a tagged turtle is somewhat on the slim side, but turtles are marked and they are occasionally stranded on the European coasts; in one bumper year there were eleven recorded in Britain alone. A metal tag may be attached to the hind border of one of the front flippers, but until now adult turtles only have been marked (by scientists in the USA and Mexico) and these are less likely to reach our shores. If ever one is found, however, it will be valuable proof of its origin. It is well known that loggerhead turtles make regular journeys into the Atlantic, and it seems likely that young turtles have on occasion been swept off course by Caribbean hurricanes, then carried to Europe by the North Atlantic Current. If this is the case, then the journey may take well over a year.

Lastly we come to the possibility of finding a stranded whale. Whales are air-breathing mammals, like seals, but in their case they are truly marine, and if you find one on the beach it is either dead or in serious trouble. On occasion they may be stranded on beaches in quite large numbers. This usually happens in the case of species which live in sociable schools, so that if a disaster happens to one it happens to the lot. There is no clear explanation for these strandings; possibly the reason is nothing more complicated than that the whales have found themselves trapped in shallow water on a falling tide. The smaller species, like dolphins, will survive for many hours, but their schooling instinct is so strong that even if some individuals are man-handled back into deep water they drive themselves back to join their mates. The larger species inevitably die when out of the water, because their sheer weight – without the support of the surrounding water – bears down on their lungs and makes it impossible for them to breathe.

Pilot whales are typical of those stranded in large numbers, while killer and other solitary species tend to get into trouble all by themselves. Some of the records are astonishing, like the two narwhals that beached by the Thames in 1949. Arctic animals, these were the first British records for 128 years.

Whales are technically Royal Fish and, as such, stranded specimens are dealt with by the Receiver of Wreck under the Wreck Regulations. Sturgeon are included in the Receiver's responsibility, but other large fish, carcasses, etc, are the province of the Public Health Officer. (In Scotland whales of the species known as bottlenose and caa'ing [pilot] and also those of a length less than 25ft [17.5m] from tip to tail, are not Royal fish and are not claimed on behalf of the Crown.)

Fishes Royal are so called because by ancient usage they were the prerogative of the King – a tithe rendered to him for guarding the seas and protecting the coasts from pirates and robbers. They belong to the Crown not only when stranded but also when caught in territorial waters. Although the practice dates back to Plantagenet times, the first recorded example in the English language is of an Elizabethan lawyer who writes in 1570 of 'great or roialle fishe, as whales or such other, which by the Lawe of Prerogative pertain to the King himselfe'. Edward I declared that the whole sturgeon was reserved for the King, but that in the case of a whale the King should have the head, the Queen the tail and the captors the carcass. But Edward II made a clean sweep and proclaimed: 'The King shall have wreck of the sea throughout the Realm'.

We may wonder what value the King received from the unfortunate whales cast ashore, but it is as well for all of us that the Crown recognises responsibility for disposal of the remains. The Royal Navy has often done the job with explosives, but it can be a difficult task, especially in remote places. Mostly they are towed out to sea and sunk.

Detailed records have been kept of stranded whales, dolphins and porpoises since 1913. In an average year, something like fifty may come ashore. Because cetaceans are difficult to study 'in the field' there has always been a keen scientific interest in the carcasses. Coastguards and Receivers of Wreck report to the Natural History Museum in London, using a specially compiled report form, which details a great deal of information about the species, size, shape, colour and other useful data.

If you are the first to discover a stranded whale, inform the nearest coastguard, he will know what to do. Do not start to extract whale meat for your pet's dinner, for you will soon have the Keeper of Zoology hotfoot from South Kensington, not to mention the Receiver of Wreck from the nearest Custom House, coming to see your find.

4

Dunes

Holiday brochures showing sandy bays bounded by romantic rocky headlands, or long stretches of golden sand entice us to leave our homes for a holiday, but once at the seaside we demand roads and car parks, railways, hotels, promenades, ornamental gardens, and all the amenities that make up a resort. So in reality a lot of our sandy beaches are backed by solid concrete.

These unyielding structures, built against the will of the sea, act just like cliffs in many ways. They rarely give a foothold to plants and animals as the natural cliffs do but, at vast expense, they stop the sandy beach from spreading inland and taking over. Given half a chance, usually during winter storms, the beach will try hard to move in on a slumbering town, clogging guest house gardens with sand and strewing boulders along the promenade. This is an affront to civic dignity, of course, and sand is swept from the streets as quickly as the wind can carry it ashore.

But if the wind carries sand beyond the beach to a tract of land that man has not claimed for promenading, then a whole new world of sand may grow up – duneland. These duneland habitats, behind the beach, can often be recognised on the map by their local names, like Newborough Warren, Braunton Burrows, the meols of East Anglia, and the links of Scotland. Conditions have to be right – the winds, the sand, the lie of the land – but when they are, a new and characteristic landscape gradually takes shape. Offshore there may be tidal sandbanks, mysterious islands of sand which seem to rise and fall with the ebb and flow of the sea. On the foreshore there will be

DUNES

occasional shingle banks, curious hummocks of a here-today-gone-tomorrow nature. Just above the high water mark great yellow dunes rise up, held together by tough tussocks of marram grass. Protected by these primary defences, the plant-rich old grey dunes loom up further back, and, as the climax to this succession, the dune system is backed by a marshy area of dune slacks, water that provides a happy hunting ground for birds, bugs and reptiles.

The offshore sandbanks make a safe, undisturbed place for birds to roost or hunt cockles, but clearly they are of somewhat restricted value, since they are regularly covered by the tide. For all that, they represent the nearest thing to 'home' for common seals. Unlike the grey Atlantic seal, which prefers wild and exposed sea caves and beaches, common seals tend to favour more sheltered places. They frequent sand and mudbanks in estuaries and the low island archipelagos of sea lochs. On the Wash, where a third of the British common seals live – more than 6,000 of them – you are most likely to see the hauled-out seals from a boat; but off Blakeney Point in Norfolk there may be fifty or sixty at a time, lying in clear view on the sandbank islands just offshore.

The seals' coats match the colour of the water, but it is always easy to distinguish the rounded shapes of their heads as they bob in the water, staring at intruders with their big round eyes. They have good eyesight, but in these muddy waters they need to rely on their acute senses of smell and hearing when they search out flounders along the sea bed. There is no shortage of food for them in these waters, and the seal population is a healthy one, maintaining its numbers in a way that seems to have been little affected by the hunting they suffered in the

Duneland habitat

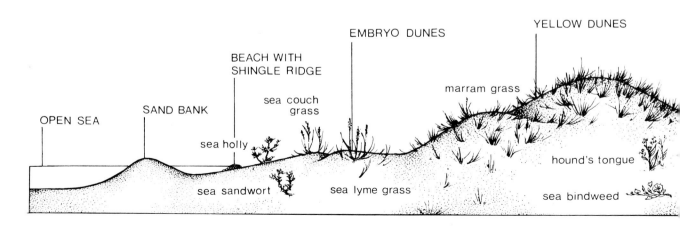

OPEN SEA

SAND BANK

BEACH WITH
SHINGLE RIDGE

sea holly

sea couch
grass

sea sandwort

EMBRYO DUNES

sea lyme grass

YELLOW DUNES

marram grass

hound's tongue

sea bindweed

past and from which they now enjoy some protection. Cyclical viral infections may occasionally reduce their numbers but in the natural course of events they may be expected to recover.

The seals settle on the banks as soon as the falling tide exposes some sand, then hump themselves down, keeping always within a reasonable panic-distance from the deep water. As the sandbank grows with the falling tide, so the number of seals increases, and soon the bank becomes criss-crossed with the 'tyre-tracks' left by the humping seals. The seals live a life half-in and half-out of the sea. They are rather slow-moving on land, but are expert divers in the water, propelled by their powerful hind flippers.

Unlike the truly sea-going whales, seals drop their young ashore. Whereas the grey seal pup spends its first few weeks passively on the beach, above high water mark and out of reach of the sea, the common seal pup must swim within hours of its birth, since it will most likely be born on a sand-or mud-bank that is uncovered for only part of the day. The young pup will follow its mother into the sea, possibly even climbing on to her back for a short ride, then it will swim through the high water period until the sandbanks begin to uncover again. The pup will receive its highly nutritious milk feed either lying at the shallow water's edge or while it nuzzles up to its mother on the drying bank. Cow and pup will recognise each other by both smell and voice. Much of their early life together will be spent lying placidly on the great mounds of sand.

That same tidal sand, drying in the wind and sunshine, sometimes moves on, to play a part in the building of duneland. Depending on the power of the wind, you may see the sand sizzling along the beach – much paler than the firmer sand

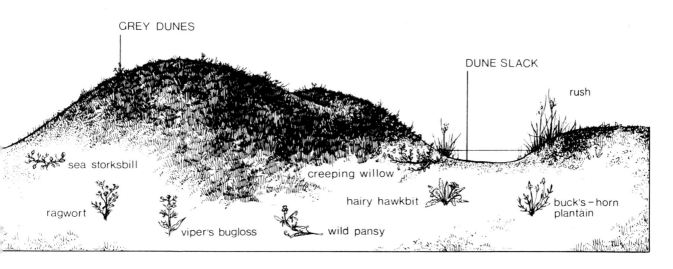

Terns: little, common, arctic, sandwich and roseate

below – and stinging your bare legs and face. A strong wind is needed to get the sand on the move, and then it progresses by a kind of jumping, known as 'saltation'. When the first grains of sand are lifted (those that are easiest to carry, probably because they are smaller or drier than their neighbours) they soon fall again because of gravity. This bump down to earth jolts the surrounding grains, making it easier for the wind to lift and move them in turn. And so the process of sand moving goes on. But it is when the movement stops for some reason and the wind drops its load, that things get more interesting. The grains may be too big to move far, the wind may suddenly lose energy, but often enough it is because an obstacle blocks its path.

A major obstacle that often confronts the runaway sand is a shingle ridge, maybe part of a spit or bar, built with material brought in from another part of the coast by longshore drift. On such spits, such as Blakeney Point, ridges of shingle may be thrown high up the beach, often during a storm when the power of the waves is sufficient to carry the stones beyond the reach of normal wave action. Sometimes these ridges continue to grow, so long as material eroded from elsewhere is available, to create very significant features on our coastline. When the wind blows, the ridges slow it down and sand is deposited on them, so that the process of dune-building begins. And those embryo dunes also provide a home for some very attractive birds.

While seals are able to breed on tidal sandbanks, breeding birds must find a place completely out of reach of the sea. Even the most salt-hardened oceanic species have to do this, for example the terns which winter off the coast of tropical Africa then come north in the summer months to take advantage of the rich fishing season around the European coasts. For terns, the ideal nesting place is a sand or shingle bank, out of reach of the waves yet within easy distance of the fishing grounds. Unfortunately these are places that people find attractive, too. The little tern, for instance, tends to nest just above high water mark, exactly where holidaymakers like to tramp. Furthermore, the bird lays small eggs, in a barely recognisable scrape-nest, in widely scattered places on the shingle, not even benefitting from the protection of a noisy colony. The crowning irony is that as a species becomes rarer – and the little tern is one of our rarest breeding birds – the incentive for egg-collectors becomes greater, so it is threatened by deliberate as well as by casual disturbance.

Trampling feet and breeding birds are mutually exclusive, so in many places the tern's best friend is an enlightened land owner. At Blakeney Point, for example, the teeming tern colonies benefit from the enlightened management of the National Trust. With the firm but friendly guidance of the wardens, many thousands of people get the chance to see nesting seabirds, but at a respectful distance. The result is that everyone benefits and the terns do very well, indeed the bird list at Blakeney Point is one of the longest for any part of Britain. Projecting into the North Sea from the Norfolk coast, the point makes a good landfall for migrants, as well as being a stronghold for the tern cities. Apart from the little terns, there are about a thousand pairs of common terns and variable numbers of sandwich terns, nesting typically close together on an embryo sand dune, almost shoulder to shoulder. This is a hazardous place to breed. The nest is no more than a saucer-shaped scoop in the sand or shingle and, quite apart from the human disturbance, blown sand or spume may bury the eggs or chicks, or an inconvenient storm may wash the whole colony away. These are natural hazards, however, and over a period of years the terns recover from them.

Other birds besides terns nest on the foreshore sand and shingle. The glossy black and white oystercatcher, or sea-pie, lives here, making an apology of a nest out of a few stones or bits of dead grass, decorated with a rabbit dropping or two. An excitable bird, the first to make its presence felt as you come round the corner, it flies around you in wide circles, peep-peeping all the time. With its long, strong, orange-red bill, it makes a living probing in the sand for cockles and shrimps. Sometimes several of the birds will join together for a curious performance in which they fly around in close company, then land on an undisturbed sandy place to continue an animated discussion, all of them piping at each other with as much power as they can muster.

Ringed plovers live in this kind of country, too. They are small plump birds, grey with a conspicuous black collar bordered with white. They nest in a sandy hollow, lined with a few stones or shells and maybe a bit of grass, laying about four eggs which merge into the surroundings, and which are vulnerable, like those of the little terns, to the passing feet of holidaymakers. When they are hatched, the baby plovers are sand-coloured and beautifully camouflaged. If you happen to walk too close to them, the parent bird will stage a masterly performance of feigned injury while the chicks crouch and freeze. Staggering about with a 'broken' wing, she will lure you – or another enemy like a marauding stoat or fox – to a comfortable distance away from the chicks, then take off and

Ringed plovers simply use a sandy hollow as a nest, lined with a few stones or shells

If a ringed plover's chicks are in danger, the parent feigns injury in the hope of luring the potential predator away

whistle her way through the air to rejoin her offspring.

Once established on a bare sand or shingle ridge, birds begin to alter the landscape. Their droppings enrich the vicinity of the nests. Bits of dead fish, an occasional dead chick and empty egg shells begin to accumulate. A humus develops, providing a place where plants can gain a foothold. The plants need moisture, and this, surprisingly enough, is supplied by the underlying shingle. If you move a few pebbles from the surface of the shingle, the lower ones are usually damp to the touch — and damp with fresh water. This water results from condensation, which in turn depends on the big differences in temperature between day and night. During a hot sunny day the pebbles heat up and the air in the spaces around them expands, but with the cool of evening it contracts again and more air is sucked down into the spaces. This newly arrived air is quickly chilled by the cold pebbles and is forced to release its moisture, much as the moisture in warm breath mists up car windows on a frosty morning. Although there is never much water available from this source, there is enough for well adapted plant species to gain a hold. That is the beauty of a plant succession. Hardy pioneers become established, flourish, reproduce, decay and make way for less demanding species. The pioneer plants of the strandlines and terneries need to be tough. The salt sea is very close, so they must be able to retain their fresh water and to resist periodic inundation. The succulent fleshy leaves of plants such as sea sandwort show just one reaction to the problem of water storage. In the case of sea holly, the leaves have a secretion of wax on their surface to help reduce moisture loss. Other plants solve the same problem by having hairy or downy leaves, a device that traps a layer of still air close to the leaf surface, helping to reduce transpiration.

These plants attract a lot of insects, which in turn provide ready-made meals for the beach birds. Under a clump of sea rocket, for instance, there will be an oasis of damp, and there the sand-hoppers will cluster. There may be flea-beetles and woodlice. All these are grist to the ringed plover's mill, and the birds will explore the sea rocket's surroundings as readily as the bumble bee will come to visit its flowers.

As a precaution against trampling, some beach plants have special protection. Sea holly is as prickly as its hedgerow namesake, and prickly saltwort lives up to its name too. Plants like silverweed and sandwort defend themselves against fierce winds and blasting sand by retreating into tight-packed rosette forms, hugging the ground, a habit that also makes passing feet less troublesome. By contrast, the flamboyant appearance of

Ringed plover searching for food under sea rocket

some of these pioneers in flower, like the yellow horned poppy, seems to belie the harshness of the environment.

These striving plants may be annoying because they prick bare toes, but by providing new obstacles to the sand-laden wind and by decaying to form more humus, they make way for the next wave of plant invasion, and with it the formation of an embryo dune. The two most important invaders at this stage are both grasses – sand couch grass and lyme grass. Sand couch grass propagates readily from seed; lyme grass – which is less common – less readily; but both spread most readily from specialised roots called rhizomes, which can tunnel under the sand and send new shoots up through it. The tall thin leaves and feathery flowers change the aerodynamic shape of the developing dune and trap sand, but it is the rhizomes that bind and stabilise the dune, casting a three-dimensional net by way of horizontal and vertical growth. The ability of sand couch grass to spread outwards horizontally is potentially unlimited, but the plant cannot tolerate great quantities of sand piling on top of it. More than about 2ft (60cm) in a year will swamp it out. By contrast, lyme grass rhizomes have been shown to grow upwards of 5ft (150cm) towards the light, and buds found 2ft (60cm) below the surface were still capable of growth. So the two grasses make a good team, especially as they can both survive an occasional dousing with salt water when storm waves or extra high tides invade the margins of their dune.

Sand couch and lyme grass continue the process of accretion, gradually building up the embryo dune until it reaches a height at which it is rarely inundated by the sea. Now the way is open for the kind of dune that most of us imagine. Quite big – big enough to jump off or slide down, and sprouting all over with a greyish spikey grass – marram grass. Marram grass cannot tolerate being covered by the sea, which is why, in the natural succession, it takes over when the other species have raised the land above the level of normal sea attack. But marram has other strengths, and is a very special plant. Unlike any other, it has potentially unlimited vertical *and* horizontal growth, again by means of rhizomes. It is the vertical ability that allows dune hills to grow tall. At 100ft – more than 30m in places – the dunes at Braunton Burrows are among the highest in Britain. Marram thrives on sand burial. When a shoot is overwhelmed by sand its reaction is to produce a bud, which develops into a new vertical shoot striving for the surface. When the light is reached leaves are formed and the whole process starts again, because the leaves and subsequent large feathery flowers trap yet more sand, by slowing down the wind which carries it.

Three pioneer grasses: A marram, B lyme grass and C sand couch; the two plants below them, D sea sandwort and E prickly saltwort, are at home on the driftline and among the dunes

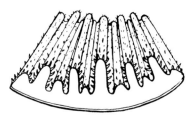

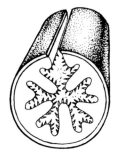

Marram grass – a remarkable plant which thrives on sand inundation: *top* underground shoots develop into leaves when they break the surface, to produce a typical pattern of tussocks; *centre* transverse section through a leaf; *bottom* stomata are located in the depressions, and become protected when the leaf rolls into a tube during dry conditions

The marram plant grows taller and more extensive as it builds its dune, and its outermost parts become more and more remote from the water which is stored below the sand. So it becomes increasingly important that the plant uses its available water wisely. Like the other pioneers, marram has special mechanisms for preventing water loss in this environment where the winds, whistling through the leaves, have a great potential for water removal. The stomata, small gaps in the cell wall through which water is lost during transpiration, are protected by being placed in depressions or grooves, sunk in the leaf surface. During dry weather, when conditions are especially difficult, the long leaves curl into a narrow tube to insulate the stomata from the drying outside air. The outer surface of the tube, which has no stomata, also aids water conservation by virtue of a thick cuticle. The greyish cast on a marram dune in summer is the result of all these curled leaves. The dramatic consequence of a shower of rain can often be seen as the leaves re-open, spreading a fresher green colour across the sand hills.

Marram grass will never completely clothe a dune. It grows in a pattern of tussocks made up of several groups of plants with lots of bare sand between. These open spaces give the name 'yellow dune' to this stage of the succession. On the open sand desert between the tussocks you are liable to find an unexpected number of spiders and insects. Some of these have been blown in by the wind, but some fly in by design. Hunting wasps find prey here. Tiger beetles and harvestmen wander about on the loose sand. There may be tracks and signs to see, for occasional hedgehogs and foxes, stoats and adders may pass this way. On a hot day there may be a common lizard basking in the sun.

In the yellow dunes, most living things are based on the tussocks of marram, where whole communities of animals find a home. Here the climate is much less severe. Much cooler inside on a hot day, much damper, more sheltered. The hunting spider *Cheiracanthium* chases his prey amongst the grasses and over the sand, camouflaged by his straw colour and grey-green abdomen to merge into the sand and marram background. In summer the female builds a cocoon by binding the tops of the grass stems with silk to make a dome, which shelters her eggs. Sand dune spiders are mostly species that are also found in marshland. On the face of it this may seem odd, but the parched surface of the yellow dune is misleading, for conditions in the heart of the marram tussocks are not arid. The surface temperature will be several degrees cooler than on the bare sand, and the grass cover preserves a pocket of still air within the tussock. The result is that the interior is always humid, and sympathetic to small creatures. Several dune spiders burrow under the tussock sand to construct silken egg cells. Others have developed long, un-spider-like bodies, and spend their days clinging head downwards to a marram stem, looking as much like a piece of stem as possible in the hope of remaining unseen. At night these jumping spiders, like *Tibellus maritimus*, *Hyctia nivoyi* and *Synageles venator*, roam the stems and sand, searching out small insects on which to pounce. One of them, *Attulus saltator*, is only found on sand dunes, whereas the others are equally at home, along with a greater variety of species, in wetland marshes. Also at night, the caterpillar of the shore wainscot moth, *Leucania litoralis*, will emerge to feed exclusively on marram spikes. During the day it lies hidden in the sand. There are snails in the dunes, too, and it is worth searching the vegetation for them, especially after a good shower of rain.

Some dune spiders have long, unspider-like bodies, resembling the marram stems, in the hope of remaining unseen

Black-headed gulls may colonise marram dunes and transform them into a noisy and sociable clubland. Whereas other gulls tend to prefer more rocky homes, on open cliffs and island clifftops, these settle for dunes, saltings, and boggy moorland pools or freshwater lakes. Marram dunes suit them well, and they build their nests, close together, on the low vegetation between the tussocks and on the tussocks themselves. A scruffy affair, the nest is woven from whatever material lies close to hand and is sufficient to provide a saucer for the three eggs. Both parents take turns to incubate and then to feed the chicks, which soon become infected by the general air of excitement and wander about from tussock to tussock, genially buffeting and being buffeted. Genial most of the time, that is, for like most gulls, the black-heads will take advantage of any opportunity, and that includes a neighbour's fat chick. It

Black-headed gull in marram grass

Caterpillars of the cinnabar moth eating the leaves of ragwort

Skylark

may also include any plover or tern chicks that offer themselves, so black-headed gulls are not entirely welcomed by the tern-conscious nature reserve warden. A gull colony may cover a considerable area of sand dune, and over a period of time the trampling and droppings will affect the vegetation. Certainly, once the yellow dunes are established, the gulls help to pave the way for the next wave of plant succession on the sheltered side, away from the immediate effects of salt spray and blowing wind.

Blown sand is the key to life for marram grass. Each layer of sand deposited on the plant stimulates it to produce fresh, vigorous shoots. But as the dune grows backwards from the sea, so the supply of sand diminishes, and the marram loses its grip, making way for a lively newcomer, sand sedge. Sand sedge thrusts up green leaves with military precision, from a horizontal rhizome which penetrates the sand in a dead straight line. And on ground enriched with rabbit and hare droppings, wind-blown tideline debris, fragments of shell, and so on, mosses and lichens also establish themselves. Hounds-tongue, storks-bill and sea bindweed and many other plants continue the work of stabilising the landward face of the dune system. Over a period of hundreds of years the 'grey' dune develops; the greyness largely due to the abundant growth of lichens. Well drained, firm and dry, this is the dune country the walker enjoys.

It is in the grey dunes that rabbits are very much at home. The well packed sand is ideal for burrowing and the dune grasses make ideal grazing, indeed the rabbits' feeding preferences determine the nature of the plant cover here, since they readily devour clovers and erect grasses but leave the ground-hugging dwarf plant forms alone. Quite apart from the droppings, which are scattered everywhere, the presence of rabbits is unmistakably shown by the typically short-cropped grass in the vicinity of the burrow entrances. They dislike getting their belly fur wet in the long grass and prefer to be near the burrow in case of emergencies. The disturbed sand around the burrow entrance is often a sympathetic holding-ground for ragwort, which does well here because rabbits are not keen to eat it. But ragwort is the preferred food for caterpillars of the cinnabar moth, which, if you find them at all, are likely to be present in large numbers.

Grey dunes are skylark country, too. A walk across the springy turf is almost always accompanied by the liquid warbling of that stout brown shape, climbing effortlessly high into the sky to proclaim ownership of the dunescape, before sinking down to the ground. Meadow pipits nest in these parts too, but their song-flights are much less musical. Looking rather similar to the skylark, they are easily told apart by their habit of sitting tight on a marram tussock, peeping plaintively if the nest is nearby.

A complete dune system may stretch back a considerable distance from the sea and this means that the valleys between successive dune ridges, known as 'slacks', are more or less insulated from wind and sea, especially the slacks between the oldest 'grey' dunes. Here the constant deposition of animal and vegetable humus allows the sand to hold more water. In the grey dune slacks, fresh water may be very close to the surface, allowing plants of damp pasture land, such as hairy hawkbit and buck's-horn plantain, to flourish. Sometimes, especially in winter, the water may even lie on the surface of the slack, forming pools of fresh or brackish water.

This system of dry dunes and wet slacks suits the shelduck, the most spectactular bird of the grey dunes, very well. A large duck, almost gooselike, it has a white body enriched with a chestnut chest band, dark green head, red bill and pink legs. The shelduck likes to nest in the well-drained dunes, often turfing a rabbit out of its burrow to establish a home underground. Once the ducklings – and there may be up to a dozen of them – are hatched, the whole family must make its way to shallow brackish water or an estuary to feed. In the dune system, the damp slacks and pools are ideal.

No dune walker's day is complete without a scramble down the side of the dune into the damp world of the slack. Here the creeping willow flourishes, a miniature forest of yellowish stems growing a foot or so from the ground. The name comes from the way the root stock creeps along just below the surface, its plentiful decaying leaves providing rich humus, helping other plants to establish themselves in this near-bog; plants like the masses of meadow buttercup, purple orchid and lady's smock. In the miniature lakes, pink water speedwell, edible watercress and water crowfoot hold sway, while rushes hold fast at the edge.

Smooth newts may be found in these ponds and, if the temperature is right, the tadpoles of a rare amphibian, the natterjack toad. Confined to a very few, well-protected localities, and suffering because of the insatiable demand people have for sandy heathland as a habitat for coastal development, the natterjack has to fight hard to survive. It has special living requirements, always a disadvantage nowadays, when the most successful animal species tend to be those with

Some colourful plants of the damp dune slacks: A lady's smock, B meadow buttercup, C purple orchid, D creeping willow, E sea milkwort

87

Small dune pond or slack

the most catholic and opportunistic tastes. Natterjacks need sandy soil in which to burrow and warm ponds in which to breed. Dune slacks are ideal.

Natterjacks are quite different from the common toad. Smaller and less warty, they have shorter hind legs – made for walking, not jumping. Grey green, with a striking yellow stripe running right down the middle of the back, their skin is less dry than in the common toad and with their greater secretion of mucus they are adapted to survive greater heat; a decided advantage in the dunes. They can dig well with their fore-limbs, throwing sand out behind them and they are good climbers. Nocturnal by nature, they will nevertheless show themselves at the burrow entrance often enough, and may well be seen at any time of the day. At hibernation time they easily dig down some 18in (.5m) into the sand, where temperature and humidity conditions are more stable, but in early summer they migrate to the dune-ponds, where they lay long strings of eggs, several thousand of them, where the water is shallow. Sadly, this often dries out at the most inconvenient time, providing yet more food for the birds.

Short-eared owls are typical of duneland and, unlike the other owls, they are diurnal. With their long wings they glide and wheel over the dunes, searching for voles. So one way and another, a lot of plants and animals find a living here. Yet it is a community that can have its life rudely shattered overnight. A dune, especially a yellow one, is a precarious sand castle, even when covered by a diverse and well-established flora.

The binding skin of dune vegetation can easily be broken. Rabbits may burrow and nibble too assiduously or people may enjoy themselves too energetically. Sliding down the steep windward face of a yellow dune is undoubtedly great fun, but it may mean that next time you arrive for a holiday the dune has disappeared. The wind will be quick to grasp the opportunity offered by even the slightest chink in the dune's defence and a small bare patch where the vegetation has been scarred can soon enlarge into a full-scale blow-out. Big blow-outs, sitting like huge bowls among the sand-hills, signal the potential instability of the system. This instability is something we should respect, because sand dunes really matter, not only to the shelducks and lizards and natterjack toads but to the people who live and work behind the beach. Paradoxically, these fragile systems play a vital role in our coastal defences. Natural protectors, they allow the influence of the sea – the spray, the sea-warmed air, and the maritime species – to penetrate inland, but keep the sea itself at bay.

If dunes are to build sound sea defences, they need plenty of building material – sand – but in some parts of England, the east coast, for example, this is in short supply, as the prevailing winds are offshore, allowing dune-building only in limited periods. The inadequacy of the dunes, coupled with the gradual sinking of the land as the relative sea level rises, is one reason why the low coasts of Norfolk are so subject to flood and erosion. Once the dune line has been breached, the sea can spread far and wide over the flat lands behind. This is what happened so disastrously in 1953, when a storm surge in the North Sea caused flooding from Yorkshire to Kent, submerging about 500sq miles (800sq km) of country. Near Lowestoft, for example, the soft cliffs were cut back 32ft – nearly 10m. That much during one storm! This shows only too clearly the power of the sea, and the archives of east coast towns are filled with lists of houses, churches , and even whole towns that founded when the sea took the upper hand.

Sometimes the natural dune defences must be breached on purpose, as happened during the last war, when sluices were opened on land at Minsmere, in Suffolk, as an anti-invasion measure. But whether the dunes are breached by man or by nature, the resulting dune lagoons are a paradise for birds. In these shallow brackish waters which have a connection, however tenuous, with the sea, enormous quantities of fish fry and insect larvae develop. Waders and ducks move in for the feast. This is where the shelduck families come to search for small crustaceans and molluscs. On the nursery shallows and mudflats they trample, scoop and scythe vast numbers of small creatures for food.

At Minsmere, the Royal Society for the Protection of Birds

has carried lagoon management to a fine art. Over a period of some twenty years they have created an environment where a thousand pairs of birds breed, and you may see fifty different species in one day. By controlling the water levels and providing carefully engineered 'scrape' islands, they have improved living conditions for such breeding visitors as avocets and terns. Bearded tits, marsh harriers and bitterns breed there, all species which have suffered drastically from habitat loss elsewhere in the country. From carefully sited hides at Minsmere the visitor may enjoy the richest birdwatching in Britain, but the real triumph is the demonstration of what can be done to the fauna and flora of a place by thoughtful intervention. Minsmere and its marvellous riches are the happy result of a lot of hard work and controlled flooding. But a mature dune system, with its hinterland of brackish lagoons, is also ripe for 'development' of a different kind. Although it represents a superb example of natural succession, rich with highly adapted plants and animals, it is a relatively simple process nowadays to reclaim it, transforming duneland into barley fields or conifer plantations. It is worthy of a better fate, and deserves its rightful place in Britain's coastal heritage.

5
Glorious Mud

Estuaries are places where rivers finally reach the sea; the Thames, Tamar, Humber, Severn, Mersey, Firth of Forth, for example – all familiar names because of their connection with great sea ports. On a map, estuaries look like an inland arm of the sea, but on the ground it is sometimes difficult to believe that they are part of the seaside at all, looking more like a brimming lake or some extra-terrestrial landscape of shimmering mud at different stages of the tide.

Estuaries have their origin far from the roar of the sea waves. On their journey to the sea rivers change from raging upland torrents, through swift-flowing streams to broad, majestic reaches. Always the flow is downward to the sea. At the end of the journey, when the river finally discharges its load of water and sediment into the ocean, there is a region where water of different origins mingles, to flow up and down the lower valley with the rhythm of the tides. The water may be of full sea-water concentration when the tide is flooding in, whereas during lower water periods the water that remains may be nearly fresh – the outflow of the river. Between these two extremes, the sea and fresh waters are mixed together, but not uniformly so. Salt water is denser and heavier than fresh, so the fresh river water may form a layer above the incoming salt of the sea. Of course some mixing does take place, and one effect of this is to further stimulate the deposition of silt. By a process known as 'flocculation' suspended sediments are attracted to each other and, clumping together, they grow bigger until they fall. The tidal mud banks begin to grow.

In the majority of British estuaries, like the Tamar, for

example, which I have known and loved the longest, the large-scale deposition of silt began with the end of the last glaciation. Before the Pleistocene Ice Age the Tamar had formed its valley, running 62 miles (100km) to the sea in Plymouth Sound, but when the ice was formed vast quantities of water were stored, frozen, upon the land, so that the sea-level dropped by as much as 200ft (60m). Because the gradient from the land to the sea was now so much steeper, the rivers flowed faster and with greater energy, so that deep gorge-like valleys were excavated. When the ice melted, the sea-level rose again all round the country, allowing the salt water to return and drown the over-deepened river mouths. Known as 'rias', these drowned valleys form the most common type of estuary.

The return of the sea meant that the rivers slowed down again and as a result they were forced to drop more and more sediment at their mouths. So much sediment, in fact, that the rias became filled with material won from the land. The great depths of this mud, over 100ft (30m) on the Tamar for example, are often revealed by test borings for engineering works like power-stations. The sea-level is still rising and sedimentation continues, ensuring that in geological time estuaries are destined to be very short-lived phenomena. All the processes of deposition are striving to raise the shimmering mud to the status of dry land.

On an estuary, more than any other part of the coast, it is possible to see these processes of deposition at work. Stay, best of all on a boat, for a day and watch the tide ebb and flood; stay for a fortnight and see the change from neap to spring tides. Best of all, stay for a year to experience the highest equinoctial tides flooding the landscape and their lowest counterparts revealing channel beds which see the sun only twice a year.

In the dynamic habitat of the estuary, plants play a star role. By helping to trap silt they form and shape the very land upon which they grow, like the sand dune species which help to build their own homes. Again, like the dune flora, the plants form a succession, from the pioneers which struggle in the most difficult conditions to the well-established and often long-lived plants which grow where the marsh merges almost imper-ceptibly with the land. The full range of habitats that produces the succession can be seen best when the tide is out. Then the remaining water (mostly fresh water which flows continuously from the river) will flow past bare, unvegetated mud-banks. In the six-hourly cycle of the tide, these banks will be exposed to the sunlight for only a short period at the end of the ebb and the beginnings of the flood – not long enough for the survival of plants, which, containing chlorophyll, need the sun to power them.

As more mud accumulates, the surface of the tidal bank will reach a threshold at which, on every tide, there is just enough light to allow plants to grow. After *Enteromorpha*, the bright green slimy-looking plant that requires submersion and cannot tolerate much exposure, the first two important plant colonists are glasswort, or marsh samphire, and cord grass. The latter has taken over in many estuaries, but glasswort, a fleshy bright green plant that looks like a miniature tree, most effectively demonstrates the way in which the plants prepare the way for a drastic change in the environment.

Unlike most of the salt-marsh species, glasswort is an annual, and the success of its little seedlings depends on the force of the tide. A strong tidal current will dislodge the shallow-rooted plants, and this same swiftness of current may stir up the sediment to such an extent that light cannot penetrate the water effectively so again the plant cannot grow. If the plant does overcome these obstacles, it will slow down the flow of water around and over it and force sediment to settle. By thus trapping the mud, the bright green forests of glasswort gradually raise the level of the mud surface until it is exposed for longer periods on every tide. More than an inch – 3cm – a year may be accreted, the rate being greatest in autumn when the glasswort has reached its greatest size. Indeed autumn is the time when all salt-marsh species are most efficient as silt traps.

The first plants to grow on the bare mud make a big impact on the landscape when the tide is out, although of course they cannot be seen when the flooding tide covers them. After this pioneer stage the most striking aspect of the plant community is the zonation, where different plant species grow in bands, or zones, according to the length of time they are submerged on every tide. An estuary with a big tidal range will support a marsh with broad, well-displayed zones – say a pure glasswort community, followed by glasswort in association with sea blite or sea manna grass, giving way to carpets of thrift and sea lavender, with pasture grasses such as sheep's fescue at the highest levels of the marsh where tidal inundation is least frequent. On a small range estuary where the difference in level between high and low water is not great, the zones are likely to be compressed and confused, with particular species adapting to their position on the marsh by changing their growth form. Sea aster, for example, with its purple flowers so reminiscent of Michaelmas daisies, may be a tall straggling plant 2 or 3ft – nearly a metre – high in places where it is

Fescue grass often forms a close turf on the estuary saltmarsh

flooded to that depth; or it may flourish as a stockier little plant in the higher levels of the marsh where inundation is not a big problem.

In reality the location of particular species is often determined by the micro-habitats of the marsh; the creeks and pools and fresh-water drainage channels which add so much to the variety of a salt-marsh, especially when seen from the air. Drainage channels on the bar mud usually take their chosen course because of slight irregularities of the surface and, once established, tend to persist when the mud is colonised by plants. The flooding tide rises first up the creek beds which, being at a lower level than the plant-covered marsh provide the first points of entry for the rising waters. The depth of the creeks that criss-cross a salt-marsh varies a great deal, but as the water which flows in them is always deeper that the water which floods the marsh itself, the flow is faster. This relatively swift flow of water favours erosion of the channel, rather than deposition of sediments, and so the creek system is perpetuated.

In this rather unstable region of the creeks, plants must adapt. Algae which manage to grow on the steep creek banks, *Vaucheria thuretti*, for example, develop a good grip on the mud by means of a gelatinous secretion. Creeks are rather bare of plant life because of the erosion that goes on, but the plant most characteristic of the creek banks is the shrub-like sea purslane, which colonises both sides of creeks, often meeting to form a bridge over the narrower channels. Sea purslane demands good drainage at root level, so the slightly raised creek banks suit it very well and its pale grey-green foliage, winding like a road through the marsh, is a clue to the whereabouts of

Sea purslane, a shrubby perennial with grey-green leaves which favours the well-drained sides of tidal creeks

Cross-section of a creek

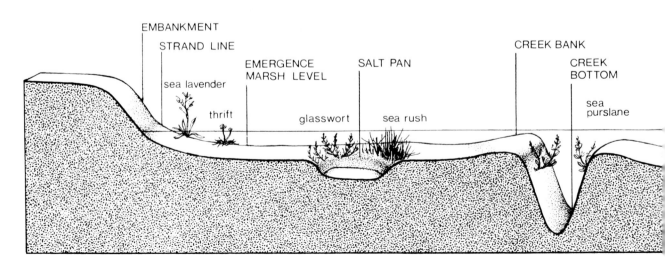

channels, that all too easily cut off the unwary marsh-walker.

As the tide rises, the channels form waterways, carrying water-borne seeds and root fragments into the upper marsh. Cord grass often becomes established in this way. Capable of reproduction from seed and from root fragments, it has such an amazing ability to accrete silt that, once it has a foothold, its vigorous growth may completely block a drainage channel. Once this happens, the way is paved for the formation of salt pans, often seen as circular depressions, where the plant species are different from their neighbours on the surrounding marsh. The salt pans begin to develop when the water of a spring tide, which covers the whole marsh and its carpet of plants, finds that its retreat is blocked by the growth of a sturdy clump of cord grass, or any other plant for that matter. The water therefore remains, becoming more and more saline as evaporation gets to work. This water may become so saline that the blocked creek section remains totally bare of plant life, like an open pond. More usually it is invaded by plants that are normally found in the pioneer zone, like the salt-tolerant glasswort or sea blite, or cord grass itself may expand to fill the entire area. These salt pans, where limiting factors like salinity and temperature become intensified, can be compared with the rock pools of the open coast.

Because they are at a lower level than the surrounding marsh, the salt pans trap and retain water with each tidal inundation, thus perpetuating the super-saline conditions. It is only when the plants have grown big and vigorous enough to trap a lot more silt that the pan may eventually be elevated to the level of the surrounding vegetation. The species most able to achieve this growth is again the ubiquitous cord grass,

GLORIOUS MUD

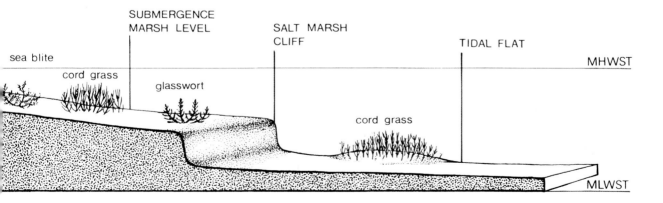

Common molluscs of the estuary:
A *Hydrobia*, B *Macoma* (Baltic tellin),
C *Cardium* (common cockle),
D *Scrobicularia* (peppery furrow), E
Mya (sand gaper)

indeed it is the super-plant of the estuary in the late twentieth century. First found in Southampton Water in the 1870s, it has spread rapidly in both directions along the south coast, and is now the major colonist, often forming neatly circular islands as it invades the bare mud. This hybrid grass is accelerating the natural process of reclamation, raising the land surface until it is almost unaffected by the tide. Man can achieve this rapidly by building dykes to keep out the flooding tide, and in Britain as early as Roman times, man was trying to increase the area of the land – notably around the Wash – by these means.

The plants that colonise the mud at the edges of the estuary must be capable of sustaining life at all stages of the tide and throughout the seasons. This same rule applies to resident animals such as the molluscs and crustaceans which, during hot summers with lots of evaporation or winters with lots of rain, must be able to cope with the great changes in salinity and still maintain a constant concentration of salts in their bodies. The common shore crab, for instance, with which we are all familiar on the open seashore, is able to thrive high up the estuaries where a good deal of its time is spent in near-freshwater conditions. When the surrounding water becomes diluted, it is able to regulate the situation by increasing the saltiness of its own blood.

The shrimps, worms and shellfish living on, and under, and at the edge of the mud, have a similar tolerance of a wide salinity range, Like their relations on the sea coast, they also take advantage of an ability to burrow down or hide under stones, which provide a more sympathetic environment. Cockles may be found in enormous numbers wherever there is sand or gravelly mud. Other shellfish which live just out of sight also thrive; on the Tamar estuary, for example, scientists have measured the Baltic tellin's numbers and say there can be nearly 600 in 1sq ft or 6,000 to 1sq m of mud. Since they inhabit the top 4in (10cm), the mind boggles at the thought of their concentration. Not surprisingly, they form a major food source, which is enthusiastically exploited by both birds and fish. Other shells, like the peppery furrow and the sand gaper, burrow deeper down and use long siphons with which to gather their surface food. Yet for all their concealment, they are not immune from attack by birds.

The smallest of all the estuary sea-shells, however, lives a good part of its life exposed on the surface of the mud. *Hydrobia* is just ¼in (6mm) long, the size of a grain of wheat, yet because of its great abundance it, too, is an important source of food for waders and ducks. Crawling over the mud, it feeds on bacteria.

I once dropped a concrete mooring-clump into the mud, only to find it swarming with *Hydrobia* shells just a few hours later, obviously enjoying the bacterial film that had already begun to grow on the freshly made concrete surface.

There may be over a hundred ragworms in a square foot (1,000 to a sq m) of mud, living in individual burrows lined with slime and emerging to feed when the incoming tide covers them. Look closely at the mud surface and you will see their tell-tale tracks in the mud, radiating from a central hole. As much as 4in (10cm) long, they have a conspicuous red blood vessel running the length of their backs. Many bait-digging anglers will testify to their possession of chitinous jaws which can give enough of a nip to hurt a finger, even if they do not draw blood. Reaching out of the burrow, they scavenge the mud around them and also take passing small crustaceans. Opposum shrimps must be a likely prey. They dart about in the shallows in large numbers at low water and on the rising tide, filter-feeding on the minute plankton plants. Another crustacean, the sand-hopper *Corophium* hauls itself out of its burrow with hooked antennae and scavenges the water-covered surface. It, too, is hunted by fish and birds. So although there are relatively few invertebrate animal species living in the demanding conditions of an estuary, they exist in astounding populations and support large numbers of visiting hunters, fish, bird and mammal.

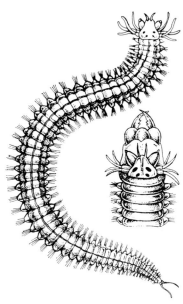

Ragworm *Nereis*, with close-up of chitinous jaws

Flounders are typical estuary fish, though they are the only flat fish to be found there. Spawning at sea, they are nevertheless able to tolerate fresh water for long periods. Hunting over the shallow mud as the tide comes in, they take cockles and tellins, shore crabs and shrimps and gobies. Grey mullet, toothless browsers, swim up on the tide to graze the seaweeds. In the autumn they will patronise yacht marinas, sucking the fringe of green weeds that sprout richly around the waterlines of boats – especially those which are rarely used. The mullet may, on occasion, take an animal larva or a small shrimp, and it is also partial to a morsel of bread – even the mass-produced variety – which makes it a fairly easy catch for the fisherman.

Eels are very common in estuaries, spending some time there during the uphill journey to the river from the Atlantic of their youth, and also on their last, downhill, journey in the silver livery of spawning. The Atlantic salmon are passage migrants, too, although their life-history is almost the exact opposite to that of the eel. Most of their adult life is spent at sea, growing fat on the rich food of the Arctic; but they return to their native

Grey mullet graze algae and often lie motionless at the surface, basking in the sun

Sanderlings haunt the very edge of the water, chasing tiny creatures revealed by the backwash (*Heather Angel*)

Turnstones do just that – they turn pebbles and weed fronds in a search for small crabs, worms and shrimps (*Roger Tidman/FLPA*)

Fulmars, now common coastal birds, are superficially gull-like, but have a thicker-set head, a darkly sleepless eye and the tube nostrils of a petrel; though they feed at sea, they spend a great deal of time patrolling the cliffs and tending their nest-ledges (*Eric & David Hosking*)

rivers to spawn. In a summer of drought, they may congregate in estuaries in large numbers, waiting for the rainfall that provides them with enough fresh water to smell their way up the rivers. This is the time when they may be taken in seine nets, and thereby denied the chance to spawn or fertilise. Never miss a chance to join the netsmen at their work and perhaps see one of these splendid fish. Look carefully at its body and, if it is fresh-run, there may be some sea-lice clinging to it. These parasites do not survive long in fresh water, so the estuary is the most likely place for you to see them. Less than ½in – a centimetre or so long – they have a hollow flattened body which acts as a suction disc, pressing against the fish skin. Two prehensile claws dig into the flesh and grip hard.

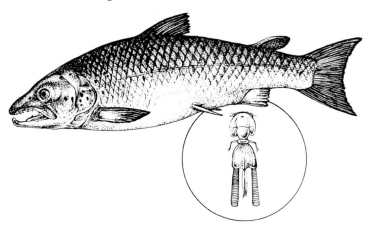

Fresh-run salmon often carry sea-lice (inset)

All these fish represent a food source for man, and they are accordingly netted, trapped and angled. They are also assiduously hunted by birds. The salmon's main enemy is certainly man, as his size makes him an unlikely prey for most birds. I have watched ospreys hunting salmon in the tidal creeks of the Westcountry in August and September, when they stop over for a few weeks on their journey from the breeding season in Scandinavia, to the wintering grounds in Spain. However, their main prey at this time seems to be mullet, which, because they spend a lot of time at the surface, make an easy catch for the fish-hawk. The osprey is a leisurely hunter, flying up and down a calm reach a few times before it decides which individual fish to swoop down and pounce on.

Eels are taken in fair numbers by the cormorants, which spend the greater part of the year living in these tidal waters. Choosing a likely area, the bird does a jack-knife dive into the rich muddy water and searches the bottom, to emerge, half a minute later, with a wriggling eel as long as himself. The struggle to swallow it may be dramatic and prolonged. Cormorants will take flounders, and these flatfish are also diligently stalked by herons. Grey herons, along with cormorants and shelducks, are typical estuary birds. Indeed, while cormorants go down to the sea for the breeding season and shelducks leave for a few months while they moult their flight feathers, the heron is the only one to stay faithful to the creeks and mudflats throughout the year.

The heron is a sociable bird whilst nesting at the heronry, and at roosting times, but is a somewhat solitary hunter. Each individual has a feeding area which he regards as his own, and he patrols the water's edge as the turning tide brings the fish fry and fat flounders within his reach. While he may spend a good deal of time standing at the water's edge, relaxed, with half an eye open, or standing with outstretched neck, leaning forward to wait for the fish to come to him, his most successful fishing by far is accomplished when he stalks actively. Wading very slowly through the shallow water he watches, and then stabs. Small fish are swallowed whole, on the spot. Larger ones are carried off to the nearest field or to the saltings, shaken and broken, then eaten at leisure. As the tide rises over the mudflats, the heron will fly majestically to join his mates, perhaps in a convenient waterside tree, or perhaps standing in a group in the middle of an undisturbed field, to preen and rest.

While cormorants and herons fish, shelducks hunt over the exposed wet mud on the ebb, as well as in the very shallow water at the edge of the tide, looking for molluscs and shrimps. Paddling across the mud, they sweep the surface with their bills, searching out the *Hydrobia* and tellins. They may also indulge in the 'puddling' which is so typical of gulls on wet sandy beaches or flooded playing fields. Puddling up and down with their broad webbed feet compacts the mud or sand, and forces both shellfish and worms to the surface.

In springtime and early summer the estuary is a fairly quiet place from the birdwatcher's point of view, because the tidal nature of the habitat means that very few birds breed there. Mute swans may build their nests on the salt-marsh, a risky thing to do, since the nests and eggs are often swept away by spring tides. Plenty of small birds may colonise the reedbeds where they can build out of reach of the tide; and there may be a few non-breeding redshanks or curlews or plovers. But at this time the vast majority of the estuary birds are thousands of miles away in the high Arctic and in Scandinavia, so it is especially good to have the company of shelducks, which do stay to breed. They will have been courting noisily since the

Waders congregate in huge numbers in wintertime on estuaries because they offer peace and quiet, a comparatively mild climate and abundant food; knot on the Dee (*Heather Angel*)

Left
After a storm, large quantities of seaweed may be cast ashore after being torn from its anchorage; coastal farmers take advantage of this rich natural fertiliser by collecting it in bulk (*Heather Angel*)

Opposite
Shelducks are typical of the estuary; they nest ashore in rabbit burrows or under bramble bushes but feed over the soft mud, mainly on small snails, *Hydrobia* (*F. Lane/FLPA*)

turn of the year; anything up to a dozen birds promenading on the mud and taking part in highly formalised dancing parties. Long before spring they have chosen a nesting-place, perhaps underground in a rabbit burrow, or hidden in the depths of a bramble bush above the marsh, and while one bird sits tight on the dozen eggs, the other will stand sentinel out on the saltings or on the fields nearby.

When the ducklings hatch, after thirty days of incubation, they must go down to the mudflats where they find their food. At one day old, they are led from the burrow by their parents, across fields, ditches, hedges, roads and all – maybe as much as 4 miles (6.5km) – though usually much less – and across the saltings to gain the safety of the mud. Inevitably, on the way, some ducklings fall prey to marauding foxes and crows. Once on the mud, the duck introduces them to the delights of ragworms and shellfish, while the drake stands guard. Gulls and crows are always ready to take advantage of an unwary duckling that strays too far from the safety of the family circle, and by the time the ducklings are a week or two old, the brood is usually reduced to half a dozen or less. Shelducks have a very loose family bond. Week-old ducklings will readily join the nearest brood or crèche when they are alarmed, and by the time they are three weeks old, they are almost independent. From then on they will mix freely with the ducklings of other families, forming a crèche with anything up to a hundred members supervised by just one pair of adults. Whether these playschool supervisors are self-appointed, chosen, or just landed with the job by virtue of being the last pair to hatch ducklings, is unclear. Certainly by the time ducklings are a month old, their parents are beginning to leave the home estuary to fly away on a moult-migration, to Bridgwater Bay or the Heligoland Bight. They join many thousands of others to find safety in numbers during this vulnerable period, when they are confined by their flightless state to sandbank and sea, while they moult and grow new flight-feathers. In the late autumn they make a leisurely way home.

While the young shelducks are perfecting their hunting in mud and shallow water, the young herons are fishing the water's edge on the rising tides, pecking at floating feathers and bits of wood as often as at a passing goby. By midsummer, the first of the returning waders begin to appear: some to refuel and pass on, perhaps to West Africa, and some to stay for the winter.

On the Tamar I expect to see the first godwits, still in their colourful breeding plumage, by about the middle of July. And

Shelduck in nest burrow

Godwits

by the middle of August there are thousands of waders, though the peak may not be reached until nearer Christmas. Waders are the birds that make estuaries such exciting places for bird-watchers, yet at first sight many of them seem almost dowdy in plumage, out of the breeding season. Their sheer numbers can be impressive, though. In Britain their mid-winter population will reach nearly a million and a half. Sometimes a shimmering mudflat will be alive with their busy bodies, advancing across the rich feeding ground like a terrible army, decimating the worms and shellfish in their path. They migrate over vast distances, from the fly-rich Arctic breeding grounds to the worm- and mollusc-rich mudflats and lagoons of northern Europe and Africa. Small to middling in size, they are gregarious and open-living characters, richly varied in their adaptations to their prey. They are master aviators, found anywhere in the world where there is a shallow patch of wet.

Waders find food by touch, taste and movement, looking for tell-tale signs and probing with bills which have a mass of sensory nerve endings. Their bills come in an astonishing variety of shapes, and the beauty of it all is that a whole host of different species can live off the same tidal mudflat because to a large extent they are hunting at different times, different levels and in subtly different habitats. While the fish and the cormorants stay in the water, the herons and black-headed gulls and some of the waders are at the water's edge, while many others spread out over the exposed mud. Dunlin, for instance, the most numerous of all, prefer wet mud, especially close to the waterline. Twisting and turning in aerial flocks, they bomb in to peck for sand-hoppers and *Hydrobia*, worms and small tellins. Clouds of knots fly in from high arctic, alternately darkening the sky and then flashing brightly as they

Curlew, calling in flight

105

Blue-rayed limpets graze on the kelp of the lower shore (*Heather Angel*)

Opposite
Rock pools are richly decorated with plants and animals – sea slug, mussels, snakelocks anemones, sea anemones, winkles, shore crab and limpets
(*Heather Angel*)

Wintering ducks (male and female) on the estuary: *top to bottom* mallard, wigeon and teal

manoeuvre on the wing. On the mud they pack together tightly in such numbers that it comes as no surprise to find that there are more than a quarter of a million of them wintering in Britain.

Redshanks, one of the common companions of any estuary day, with their noisy 'tew' calls and their white wing-bar, are in competition with the others for worms and sand-hoppers, but they have a preference for tidal pools and the water's edge. With a brisk walk and an occasional dash, they peck, jab and 'mow' the surface. It has been calculated that a redshank may peck up to 40,000 times a day in pursuit of a full stomach. The much less common greenshank also likes to chase shrimps and small fry in tidal pools, whilst the godwits, black-tailed and bar-tailed, choose to work slowly and methodically over the open mud, heads down and bills busy, feeling the texture of the mud and extracting tellins and worms. With their longer bill they can reach down into the mud for the larger shells, 4in (10cm) under the surface.

Curlews are everyone's favourite, with their long down-curved bills and that lovely liquid cry. Solitary, or in parties of mixed company, they stand out by virtue of their size, as largest of the waders. Strolling over the mud, they pause to probe, then maybe run several metres to pick up an unwary ragworm. With a beak reach of some 6in (15cm) they have free choice of all the mud creatures, even reaching down to the peppery furrow shell. While they may not quite reach down to the lugworms in the bottom of their chambers, they can and do catch them by the tail as they reach up to expel detritus in the worm cast. Cockles and other shellfish are swallowed whole, the indigestible shells subsequently rejected in the form of a pellet. On the upper shore, especially in autumn, they hunt the abundant shore crabs by sight, rather than by touch and taste.

Other birds visit the estuary in spring and autumn as passage migrants, like the osprey for instance. The odd spoonbill may show up for a few weeks or even stay the winter. Terns, which may have bred on the south and east coast or in the inland marshes of central Europe, come to fish for a few weeks before passing on to congregate in the Irish Sea, the Wash or the Moray Firth.

Swans, ducks and geese, which may have bred thousands of miles to the north and east, migrate to enjoy Britain's milder winter weather. The harder the weather, the further south they penetrate. So whereas in a mild winter the Westcountry may see only mute swans, a harsh winter in the north will soon present us with an influx of Bewicks and whoopers as well.

Many thousands of wild ducks arrive to patronise the saltings, where they find winter supplies of seeds, carried down by the rivers and deposited on the salt-marsh at high water. The abundant seeds of sea purslane and other marsh plants are also welcome. Mallards, wigeon and teal are the commonest.

Geese are birds of the saltings, too. They may fly inland to graze the barley fields, but they return to the wide open marshes to find safety for roosting. In Scotland and the northern half of England, while the whitefronts come in thousands, the greylags and pinkfeet come in tens of thousands. The most maritime is the brent goose, which feeds on the low-water beds of eel-grass in the lower estuary, although it will also graze the green seaweeds and take the occasional mollusc or shrimp.

Apart from the birds, a fair number of mammals visit the estuary from time to time. Foxes, rabbits and grey squirrels hunt and graze the saltings; otters fish and mink haunt the tidebanks looking for anything that moves. Grey seals chase salmon and common seals chase flounders. If conditions are favourable, allowing peace and quiet, the seals may lie out on a lower water mud bank or an isolated rock many miles from the sea and wait for the returning flood. However, when small whales venture high into the narrowing creeks they run the risk of being stranded. Porpoises are often seen in the estuary waters, perhaps chasing mackerel shoals. Bottle-nosed dolphins and killer whales may venture into the muddy waters, too, looking for salmon, so these 'barren' wastes turn out to be important feeding grounds for a long list of hunters.

Estuaries are wild, sometimes alien and forbidding places, but they have a richness of life and a constantly changing pattern of life and texture that creates a strong attachment for those who come to love them. The tidal and seasonal comings and goings of birds, in wheeling flocks, serve always to underline the importance of the mud and salt-marsh as providers of food.

Because they seem such deserted places to the uninitiated, they face continuous assault by developers. The mud and salt-marsh acres seem fated to exploitation by water barrage or drainage engineers, and those who seek to build oil, airport and dock installations. This ecosystem, one of the most naturally fertile in the world, combining nutrients from both land and sea, is highly vulnerable to the terrible power wielded by man, the arch-despoiler. The fragile green shoots of glasswort may pioneer a mighty salt-marsh, but they cannot resist the 'improver' without a bit of help.

GLORIOUS MUD

Wintering wild geese: *top to bottom* greylag, pinkfooted, whitefronted, brent; brent geese feed on estuary eel-grass, while the others fly inland at night to forage in fields

Opposite
The peregrine is king of the cliffs, preying on almost any other coastal bird; the nest is usually on a ledge with a commanding sea view (*R. Austing/ FLPA*)

Choughs are the most specialised of the crow family; they are coastal birds, foraging for grubs and worms on the clifftop, but nesting on impossible cliff ledges or in cave entrances (*John Hawkins/Eric & David Hosking*)

6

Hard Rock

The rocky coasts of Britain appear timeless. Unlike shifting sandbanks, bars, shingle ridges and sand dunes, which may present a new picture on every visit to a favourite beach, the rocky shores seem permanent and unchanging. It is only when you witness a cliff fall, or marvel at the unblemished surface of a slate freshly separated from the parent rock, that you realise that erosion is continually happening. For our rocky shores are the product of erosion.

The surface of our island is under constant attack from the elements, but on the coast this attack is intensified, as battle can rage on the open cliff faces as well. Rain, wind, frost and ice are powerful agents of land-based erosion, causing cliffs to slump and blocks to fall, but on the coast the sea adds its weight to the campaign. The sea also plays an important role as an agent of transport, clearing away the fallen debris and so providing destructive waves with renewed opportunities to act upon a fresh cliff face. The sea has several methods of attack. When, in deep water, waves reach to the base of a cliff, the hydraulic pressures exerted can be enough to split open the rock, especially in a well jointed structure. Air, which is trapped in joints and crevices, is compressed by the oncoming wave, and the sudden release of pressure caused by the retreating water acts like an explosion, forcing rock to shatter. Rock fragments prised from the cliff in this way, then join the wave's armoury, to be hurled back powerfully, adding insult to injury.

In the shallow water, where waves roll and scrape the loose material over the solid rock of the foreshore, a relatively level rock bench known as a 'wave-cut platform' is formed. The continuous swash and backwash sculpts and smooths the rocks in a relentless effort to reduce the land to a uniform level. But marine erosion is highly selective. The more varied the rocks, the less regular will be the coastline. On the large scale, resistant formations stand out as headlands or islands, while the more easily eroded material gives way to bays. On the local scale, joints, bedding planes and small variations in geology ensure that some rocky foreshores are almost uniform and smooth, whilst others like the marvellous hexagonal blocks of basalt on the Isle of Staffa, or the castellated granite of Land's End, loudly proclaim their geological origins.

A sandy beach is always enjoyable, whether the tide is in or out, but when the tide goes down on a rocky shore, it leaves a landscape that, at first sight, is not very enticing. Seaweeds render the rocks slippery and difficult to negotiate, barnacles seem to be just waiting to scrape an unwary knee, there are holes to fall into and crevices to trap imprudent feet. Nevertheless, for more than a century this kind of country has been recognised as a wonderland for wildlife hunters – ranging from the small child seeking crabs for his bucket to the serious seashore naturalist.

During the early nineteenth century, when people were

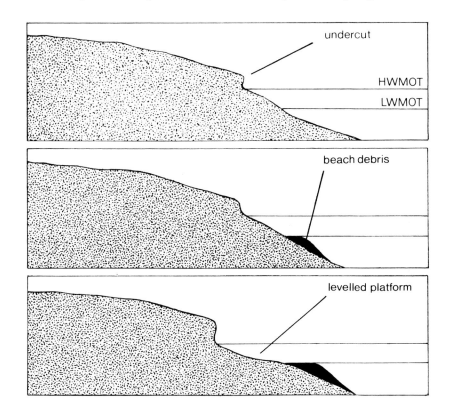

Waves act most powerfully between high and low water mark, in an effort to reduce this area to a level wave-cut platform

113

A rabbit surveys its island kingdom;
the close-cropped turf is clear evidence
of rabbit grazing (*Heather Angel*)

Opposite
Wild cabbage flourishes on this Dorset
cliff; our domestic cabbage is directly
descended from this wild stock
(*Heather Angel*)

Top to bottom Channelled, spiral, bladder and knotted wrack

discovering for the first time the joys of running free on the sand and bathing in the health-giving salt water, another kind of joy was being found by people who were caught up in the enthusiasm of a very special naturalist, Philip Henry Gosse. Gosse, born in 1810, grew up with an intense interest in nature. He nurtured his interest during his early career, which took him to America and Canada, first as a clerk then a teacher. His first book, *The Canadian Naturalist*, started him on a lifetime of writing that combined his great talent for descriptive prose with his ability as an artist. His travels abroad were halted by ill health, and it is fortunate for us that he chose to settle and work in England, in the seaside town of Ilfracombe. His joyous writing opened people's eyes to the wonders of inter-tidal life, and many were able to experience his enthusiasm at first hand as they followed him on conducted tours over the foreshore.

At the head of the procession, like Apollo conducting the Muses, my father strides ahead in an immense wide-awake, loose black coat and trousers, and fisherman's boots, with a collecting-basket in one hand, a staff or prod in the other. Then follow gentlemen of every age . . .
(Edmund Gosse)

Gosse's great achievement was as a populariser, but although he may be the best-known of the Victorian enthusiasts, he was certainly not alone. Mrs Alfred Gatty, who wrote *British Seaweeds* in 1863, spoke of seaweed collecting as a pursuit . . .

. . . which throws a charm over every sea-place on the coast . . . Only let there be sea, and plenty of low, dark rocks stretching out, peninsular-like, into it, and only let the dinner hour be fixed for high-water time, and the loving disciple asks no more of fate.

In the last quarter of the nineteenth century, interest in the living inhabitants of the rock-pools and rugged shores waned in favour of shell collecting and visits to the many shell grottos which sprang up along the coast. Today, happily, more and more people are discovering the pleasure of getting their faces close down to the slippery rocks and shining pools.

The range of living things you will find on a rocky shore will be greatly influenced by the amount of shelter available. Clearly a rocky bastion, taking the full brunt of the Atlantic attack, will have fewer animals and plants to show than the sheltered ledges inside the horns of a great bay. The degree of exposure to sunlight, the salinity, temperature and the effects of man-made pollution will be important factors too, but the most profound influence is that of the tide. Rising and falling twice in a period of just over a day, the tide, with its fortnightly cycle of high-range springs and low-range neaps covers and uncovers the rocks with its periodic gift of nutrient-rich water. At sea, living creatures must solve the problem of visiting or remaining near the surface to enjoy the life-giving properties of sunlight. On the shore, sunlight is always present but plants and animals must suffer the disadvantage that the food-bearing sea is available only on a periodic basis.

Though the inter-tidal area is not very deep from top to bottom, it supports a well-defined pattern of plants and animals, ranging from those that exist almost as land animals around the high water mark of spring tides, down to those that only very occasionally show their faces to the open air at the low water mark of the spring tides. Local conditions may vary the limits of this zonation. For instance, on exposed cliffs the effects of waves may send splashes of sea water high up the face to allow some hardy weeds and winkles to survive in what is known as the 'splash zone'. If you examine a sheltered rocky face like, for instance, a man-made embankment along the shore of an estuary, the life-zones are displayed with great clarity, ranging from the orange lichens representing the lowest land plants, by way of the rim of black lichen, which looks so uncannily like the effect of oil pollution and is the representative of the uppermost sea plant, down through a whole range of different seaweeds, to the lower-water kelps.

The main factor that decides where a species lives is the length of time the rocky shore is exposed to the air. Some seaweeds are adapted to a life lived almost totally in the air, while others can survive only a very occasional period out of

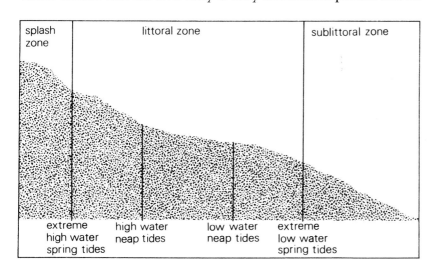

The inter-tidal area

117

Juvenile cormorant wing-drying.
Cormorants are superb divers, but it is
part of their adaptation to diving that
they have plumage which is less
waterproof than other birds; after a
fishing session they must dry their
feathers to return them to flying and
insulation trim (*Michael Rose/FLPA*)

The puffin's parrot beak is a seasonal ornament, indicating a bird of breeding maturity and potential (*Heather Angel*)

Serrated wrack *Fucus serratus*, the long front of sugary wrack *Laminaria saccharina*, and two kelps, *Saccorhiza polyschides* and *Laminaria digitata*

the sea. Unlike land plants they have no roots, for the very good reason that there is no soil for them to dig into. Their style is to grip tight to the rocks by means of a 'holdfast', and to derive their nourishment from the surrounding sea water. Like land plants, they contain chlorophyll and are able to form energy-rich sugars by photosynthesis. As *algae*, seaweeds do not flower, but propagate themselves mostly by releasing spores, which free-float in the sea until they form an attachment to some convenient surface. They represent one of the most abundant and under-exploited food sources still left to us on this planet.

There are three main groups of seaweed – green, brown and red. They are found more or less in that order, working down the shore. The seaweeds dominating the rocky shore are those that derive their brown colour from the pigment *fucoxanthin*. Like most seaweeds, they are best seen on a sheltered shoreline, where they are least bothered by the mechanical effects of wave action. At the top of the shore, around high water mark and as high as the salt spray reaches, is where you will find the dense tufts of channelled wrack. To survive long periods of exposure, its grooved fronds hold moisture while the weed dries and blackens on the surface. Specially adapted to live with only periodic submersion, this plant dies if it is kept underwater experimentally.

The next step down the shore brings you to a spiral wrack with its slightly twisted and branched fronds. At the tips of the fronds there may be swollen yellow 'sultanas', the fruiting organs. Then comes bladder wrack, one of the species with great eye-appeal because of its highly poppable air-bladders. These are arranged in pairs, whereas knotted wrack, a weed often found in close company on the middle shore, has somewhat larger bladders which are placed singly. Knotted wrack prefers more sheltered waters, whereas bladder wrack can thrive in the face of a certain amount of wave-thrashing, when the buoyancy of the gas-filled bladders holds the plant up and prevents it from being smashed against the rocks. By floating the weed upwards towards the sun this buoyancy also extends the time available for photosynthesis. Examine the wrack closely and you will often find that some of the 'bladders' are in fact cunningly shaped winkles. Lower down the shore is the home of serrated wrack which has, as its name suggests, toothed margins to the flattened fronds. Look closely at this one and you are very likely, especially if it is a well-established plant, to find the coiled, off-white tubes of *Spirorbis*, one of the bristle worms.

The largest of all the weeds live on the lower shore, the region of the kelps, the *Laminaria* family. Most of the time they are out of sight, underwater, but it is worth going to the shore at an equinox, the time of the lowest spring tides, to enjoy the sight of the edge of the forest of kelps exposed to the air. If the water is clear, allowing sunlight to penetrate and stimulate plant growth, then this weed jungle may stretch away into the submarine distance, perhaps reaching down to 30 metres, the edge of the ocean. The long single fronds of sugary wrack for example, may form a crumpled ribbon about 5ft (1.5m) long. This kelp is the seaweed beloved by amateur weather forecasters as a humidity indicator. As a natural protection against desiccation the plant is slimy and hygroscopic, attracting water, so that if the atmosphere is damp with incipient rain the frond becomes soft and limp. It has the slight disadvantage of a tendency to confirm the weather you have, rather than to forecast the weather that is around the corner! When dry, it reveals a white coating, sweet to taste, as evidence of the presence of a sugar alcohol, mannitol. In fact it has high food value, like many seaweeds, and is still used as a horse and pig fodder in places such as Iceland and northern France.

Kelps of various shapes crowd the lower-water shore, with their leathery straps and stipes, and they represent a potential food source of massive proportions, diminished only by the extreme difficulty of harvesting. Notwithstanding all the problems, these marine weeds have been and still are much used in the agricultural and chemical industries. Comparable in food value with meadow hay, weeds such as the tangleweed and the wracks are fed to horses, cattle, sheep and pigs. As fertiliser, great quantities of storm-tossed kelp are spread on coastal fields and gardens. Rich in nitrogen and potassium, kelp is good for potatoes and tomatoes, but its value is restricted by the cost of transport.

A factory for the production of seaweed manure was built in the United States as long ago as 1870, and commercial companies are still marketing sophisticated liquid versions. Recent research has shown that seaweed products increase the uptake of plant nutrients, impart a degree of frost resistance, and make plants better able to withstand the attack of certain fungus and insect pests. Claims that had been considered extravagant were in fact substantiated. It seems likely that there is going to be a considerable growth in the seaweed industry as soon as factory methods can be developed to culture algae as a source of protein.

HARD ROCK

Overleaf
Guillemots are members of the auk family, which includes razorbills and puffins; it is a characteristic of auks that they breed in dense colonies (*Eric & David Hosking*)

Grey seals are inshore fish-feeders, dropping their pups in autumn on remote beaches and in caves. Fed by their mothers with rich milk, the pups (this one is three or four days old) put on weight at a phenomenal rate. Abandoned at one month of age, they fast awhile and then venture out to find their own living, often travelling great distances in their first years of life (*Tony Soper*)

Killer whales are not uncommon inshore in British waters, especially off the western coasts (*C. Carvalho/FLPA*)

In the old days, collecting *Laminaria* and *Fucus* (variously known as kelp, oarweed and tangleweed) and manufacturing kelp was a major industry in some remote islands. In Orkney, for instance, 20,000 men were employed for the whole of the summer. The weed was collected, dried in the sun and then burnt in shallow pits. While the mass was still hot it was sprinkled with water to break it up. From about 20 tons of the wet weed the result was about one ton of hard dark grey ash. Sodium carbonate and potash were subsequently extracted. The soda was used in the manufacture of glass and soap, while the potash was sold as fertiliser.

The British kelp industry went into a decline after the Napoleonic wars, when the ash was more cheaply imported from France, but it revived after the discovery of iodine in 1811. For a long time kelp was the only source, although the preparation was fraught with difficulties. If the untreated weed was washed by rain, for instance, nearly 90 per cent of the iodine was lost.

If you are collecting seaweed for your garden, the best time to do it is after a summer storm, when great quantities of rich kelp will have been torn from its anchorage and piled up on the shore. Transport it and use it before rain reduces its value.

As a direct food, seaweed is a staple item of diet in China and Japan. Full of vitamins, good for you but, it has to be admitted, unexciting to taste. In the food industry seaweed is an important source of alginates, organic substances used in an astonishing variety of ways: as an emulsifier in soups, in soft drinks, confectionery, jellies, puddings and ice-cream. It can even be transformed into the thin film used to form an edible sausage 'skin'. From the red seaweeds the chemical industry extracts agar, a gelatinous material used in bacteriological work, and vast quantities of iodine have been extracted from the brown seaweeds.

Strictly speaking, kelp is a word that applies to the burnt ash of *Laminaria* and *Saccorhiza*. In the past, a sizeable labour force, especially in northern France, was employed in burning these weeds to produce kelp for the soda which was subsequently extracted to be used in the glass-making industry. *Saccorhiza*, unlike *Laminaria*, is an annual weed, but nevertheless it grows to an astonishing length. Commonly 6½ft (2m) long, in one year it may stretch as much as 13ft (4m) from the tips of its fingery fronds to the bulbous and warty holdfast. In spite of its great size, it is (like all the seaweeds) very flexible, able to bend with the wave action and avoid breaking. At the end of the year *Saccorhiza* dies naturally, to be cast up on the beach by winter

A variety of egg shapes: *top to bottom* cluster of common whelk, flasks of netted dog whelk, ribbon of sea-lemon, string of sea hare, collar of necklace shell and mermaid's purse of lesser spotted dogfish gales, but other weeds, like the oarweed, *Laminaria digitata*, are perennial and may endure for several years unless they are much damaged by nibbling animals such as the blue-rayed limpet.

The blue-rayed limpet is a miniature snail with a translucent shell decorated with rows of brilliant blue spots, which specialises in eating into the fronds and stipes of *Laminaria*. Carving itself a shaped hollow, it spends the summer on the upper reaches of the weed, then migrates down into the holdfast in late autumn, conveniently in time to avoid the probable consequences of its own action: the weakened stipes being snapped and carried away by a storm.

Holdfasts, especially those of oarweed, are a sanctuary for many animals, and even other seaweeds. Sponges and hydroids, sea-mats, sea-squirts and crabs all congregate in the many-branched fastness, to enjoy a measure of safety from marauding predators. This is the sort of place where you are likely to find the tiny long-clawed porcelain crab, a pale and flattened creature with a belligerent pair of prize-fighter's pincers. There may be a whole collection of the eggs of different sea animals, from the flash shapes of the netted dog whelk to the cluster of sandy coloured capsules of the common whelk. The porcelain crab may even hide among the whelk capsules.

The most elegant of eggs is the mermaid's purse, deposited by the lesser spotted dogfish and secured to the kelp or wrack by a strong corner frond. Carefully packed into the purse is the young fish and his supply of yolk, enough to sustain his growth through an incubation period of seven or eight months, a time that allows the fish to attain an advanced state of development before it hatches. These creamy egg-purses are not difficult to find, and often enough they can be seen completely out of the water on an exceptionally low tide. This is the time to look for the 'sea hedgehog', too, the spiny sea urchin which grazes the sub-littoral rocks and weeds, moving slowly but surely on its hundreds of sucking tube-feet. Look carefully at the sides and underhangs of the low-water rocks to find the British cowries mentioned in Chapter 3.

While the tide is out, the seaweeds lie down, covering the rock faces and boulders like a blanket. Though the sun and wind may dry the surface of the weed, the effect is only skin deep. Draw back the curtain and you will find that it has insulated a dank and dark area, a happy home for crabs and snails and even fish. Gobies and butterfish will sit out the low-water period in energy-conserving peace and quiet. Various sea urchins will be grazing. So don't forget to close the curtain.

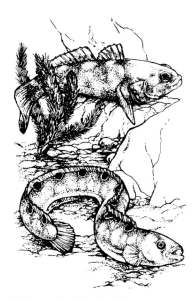

Goby (top) and butterfish

125

Mackerel are fast sea-going fish which
prey on planktonic animals, and are
themselves taken by plunge-diving
gannets (*D. P. Wilson/Eric & David
Hosking*)

Opposite
Gulls follow fishing boats for the offal
which is thrown overboard; fishing
methods and activities have great
influence on seabird populations,
sometimes to the birds' advantage,
sometimes quite the opposite (*Heather
Angel*)

HARD ROCK

On the face of it, the most effective way of sitting out the low water period is for an animal to find its way to a rock pool – an oasis of calm sea water – but life is not so simple, and in this wild aquarium there are problems. The sun may evaporate the surface water and concentrate the salinity. Or on a rainy day the pond will become diluted. If the pond is well supplied with seaweed then there will be a surplus of carbon dioxide at night and of oxygen by day, to say nothing of small boys with jam jars. So it is clear that a shallow pool, especially if it is on the upper shore, will be less rewarding than a deep one on the lower shore, replete with crevices and overhangs. Pool-watching is very good sport, and while the steadily increasing temperature during the day makes it uncomfortable for the fishy inhabitants, it is highly desirable to the casual snorkeller. Lying quietly on the surface, with your mask firmly in place, you have a window on another world. But do remember the one important rule for snorkellers – take a good strong breath every now and then, to give the tube a spring clean and to expel any carbon dioxide that has built up.

Pools are the best place to watch sea anemones, because there they are more likely to be expanded than those left high and almost dry by the tide, when their mouth openings are firmly closed to retain moisture. The scientific name of their class is *Anthozoa*, meaning flower animals, and what an apt description this is, for the various species display an astonishing range of shapes and colours. They are relatively simple animals, with no respiratory organs, as they take in oxygen through their surface tissues. They live attached to the rocks (or, in some cases – mobile homes – on the hard shells of crabs) by a slimy disc on which the animal can move about very slowly, although most of the time it simply sits still and holds tenaciously to its anchorage. The stout muscular body column is expanded at the top to display a series of hollow tentacles circling the central mouth. The tentacles wave to entice small fish or crustaceans within range of the stinging cells. Once seized, the small creature is enfolded in the tentacles and the stinging cells (*nematocysts*) keep the prey paralysed while the anemone's digestive juices get to work. Introduce your fingertip to the waving tentacles and the physical contact will trigger the stinging cells and you will feel a stickiness on your finger ends, but that is as far as the anemone's attack will go. Before it actually starts to eat your finger it needs a chemical cue to bring the feeding mechanism into play. Since a finger is not regarded as a suitable meat course by the anemone, the cue will not be forthcoming.

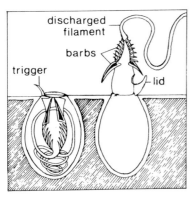

The stinging cells of a sea anemone, much enlarged

128

Hermit crab and attendants

Most of the anemones are sedentary creatures, more or less stuck to the home rock, but individuals of some species sometimes develop a working relationship with the hermit crab. By making its home base on the crab's shell, the anemone has the advantage of being carried effortlessly about so that it can lean over and sweep up the crumbs after the crab has finished its meal. The relationship has mutual advantage, in that the crab gains some protection from its close proximity to those stinging cells. Quite apart from the anemones, there may be tube worms and sponges and colonisers on the hermit crab's shell. Tucked up inside with him may be a ragworm, also taking advantage of the safety and the free transport to new feeding grounds, and paying its way by aerating and cleaning up the shell interior to the crab's benefit.

The creatures living with the hermit crab might just as easily have settled on the more conventional rock surface, and indeed the vast majority do so. One of the most striking features of a good rocky shore is the way in which every possible surface is covered with weeds and snails of one sort or another. One of the most numerous settlers is not a snail at all, although at first sight it looks like one. The acorn barnacle is a crustacean, closely related to the crabs and shrimps. Its final phase of life is on the shore, often in such numbers that you cannot avoid walking on them (indeed they make rock clambering a good deal safer, their rough shells offering such a good grip), but the animal starts life in the fashion of the other, more conventional crustaceans, free-floating in the plankton. While the others mature into the free-ranging life of a shrimp or lobster or crab, the barnacle comes to rest on a suitable hard surface. Though this might well be the shell of a hermit crab or the carapace of a crawfish – or Southend Pier for that matter – the most likely place is the rocky shore, somewhere in the inter-tidal area.

Once arrived, the barnacle cements itself firmly to the rock, and grows a conical shell of limy plates that interlock to protect the body and also provide a hinged *operculum* at the apex. This opening, through which the barnacle feeds, closes when the tide recedes and the animal is exposed. When the sea, with its charge of plankton food, surrounds the barnacle, it opens the trap door and six pairs of feathery legs emerge to sample the passing life, combing any food items towards the open door. You can see this happening in any rock pool, but the most effective study technique is to find a barnacle-encrusted crab and introduce it temporarily to a plastic box aquarium.

Acorn barnacles survive perfectly well on the upper shore, withstanding long periods of exposure, but in these conditions, with relatively short feeding periods, they are slow to grow. On the other hand, upper-shore barnacles tend to live perhaps half a dozen years longer than those which colonise the lower levels. The great advantage of settling on the lower shore is that the tide cycle allows longer feeding time and shorter exposure, but there is more competition for home sites. The long-term result is that lower shore barnacles cluster close together and grow tall, a form of high-rise development in which the average life span is some three years.

Many marine molluscs forage and graze over the surface rocks and boulders. Whereas those of sandy shores are mostly bivalves, those of the rocks and hard surfaces impervious to burrowing are mostly single-valved, gastropod snails. Instead of burrowing down to safety, they develop strong predator-resistant shells and some, like the acorn barnacles, guard the inevitable opening with the *operculum*, a sort of trap door attached to the foot-muscle, which can hold the door shut when required. The universally familiar and common dog whelks, which often live in exposed situations, are quite strong enough to be rolled about in a rough sea without being broken, but they are careful to deposit their eggs on the sheltered underside of stones and in crevices to protect them from the full fury of the sea. Clustered in these places, the mated pairs will produce two or three hundred capsules, most of them infertile and destined to serve as food for the few little snails that do emerge some four months later. Soon enough the baby snails range over the lower shore as active carnivores, searching for worms to eat. Dog whelks come in a wide range of colours, from off-white and yellow through to banded browns, and it may be that the assortment of colours they display is related to the particular food they are taking at the time.

The preferred prey of the dog whelk is the acorn barnacle

which is so thickly concentrated on the rocks. In order to penetrate the limy shells the whelks exude a poisonous secretion, *purpurin*, that relaxes the barnacle's muscles, allowing the whelk to force open the opercular plates and attack the flesh. Purpurin is a substance common to the *Muricidae* family, of which the dog whelk is a member, and which includes the spectacular tropical *murex* shells. Large numbers of these were collected in Roman times, in order to extract the yellow purpurin which, under the action of the sun, produced the purple dye used to edge the splendid toga of an Emperor. Imperial, or Tyrian, purple was also used by medieval monks to illuminate manuscripts.

The dog whelk, unconscious of its noble connections, has a different method for dealing with limpets as prey. Limpets are firmly attached to the rock face and have the single shell of a gastropod mollusc, far less susceptible to attack than the crustacean barnacle. The whelk climbs up on to the selected limpet and settles down to bore a neat hole through its shell, using the rasping surfaces of its belt-like tongue, a process that might take up to two days. When the long job is over, its questing proboscis enters the limpet to suck out the flesh.

Limpets are one of the commonest snails of the rocky shore. Like the barnacles, they settle on the most open surfaces, yet the two animals are not in competition. In fact, the result of the limpets' grazing is helpful to the barnacles in that it provides them with areas well cleaned of algae on which to settle. In turn, the limpet may graze over the algae growing on the barnacles. The limpets leave their home base for the grazing as soon as the tide covers their rock, or even while they are still exposed to the air if the weather is wet and cool. Ranging over some 3½ft (1m), they rasp away at any fresh growth, the favoured food being newly settled seaweed spores. At high water they return home, perhaps following their own mucus trail. Home is an exact spot for each individual, because in order to avoid desiccation when the tide is out, the margins of the shell must make a sealed contact with the rock, to retain the necessary spoonful of water inside. If the rock is of a soft nature, the limpet will grind it to make an exact fit. If it is hard, then it is the shell that is ground down to conform with any irregularities.

The limpet is wonderfully adapted for its life-style. With its broad base and cone shape it is able to deflect the force of the waves on the open shore, and its armour-plating protects it from attack by most birds, provided it has enough warning for the foot muscle to get a really firm grip on the rock. One bird that can penetrate the limpet's armour is the oystercatcher,

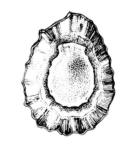

Oystercatchers have strong bills capable of dislodging limpets; they are careful to attack at the mollusc's head end (top of drawing) where the muscle attachment is least strong

131

which takes advantage of the fact that there is a weak point in the snail's attachment to its own shell. If you look inside a freshly empty limpet shell, you will see a horseshoe shaped ring, revealing where the foot muscle joined the shell. The open end represents the head cavity of the animal, and this is the end where the oystercatcher attacks, since it is least strongly held to the rock. When the shell is inhabited, the head end is easy to distinguish because the cone shape is slightly lopsided, with a steeper incline at the head. The oystercatcher takes a look, then makes a sideways thrust with its bill at the margin of the shell. Often enough the limpet is dislodged, to be carried off by the oystercatcher, which proceeds to chisel the meat from the shell. If the beak-blow should break the shell, the oystercatcher simply inserts its bill into the fracture and levers the snail off the surface of the rock. Empty limpet shells, rifled of their living contents, are often found on the tideline, with the tell-tale jemmy marks of the oystercatcher's beak around the margin, or the neatly drilled entry hole made by a dog whelk.

Dog whelks themselves are not immune from attack. Their shells may be found with the apex removed, the work of the shore crab, or with the shell smashed open completely by the powerful claws of an edible crab or possibly even a lobster. Larger holes in common whelks may be a clue to the work of herring gulls, especially when they are found well above the shoreline on a road or embankment where they have been dropped.

Unfortunately for the molluscs, these are not the only ways in which they are attacked. Waders, flatfish or echinoderms may swallow them whole and kill them with digestive juices, ejecting the inedible shell; starfish may force them to open; they may be dropped from a height by herring gulls. Yet they survive in uncountable numbers. Even when the tide is in, they are not left in peace by the birds. Eider ducks visit the shallow water of northern Britain and dive not only for a beakful of the green weeds but also to pick up small crustaceans and molluscs. Other birds, such as auks and shags, dive to chase small fish over the rocky ledges. The merganser for instance, has a specially designed saw bill that is capable of gripping even a slippery customer like the butterfish. Curlews and whimbrels enjoy rooting about the exposed weedy rocks for sand-hoppers and snails, while rock pipits and other small birds try their luck for flies and yet more sand-hoppers in the wave-tossed weed at the edge of the water. Perhaps the most typical shore-bird is the turnstone, a wader that lives up to its name by searching and

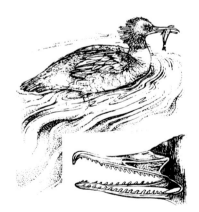

The merganser has a saw bill which is specially designed for securely gripping fish

turning the weeds and stones. Sociable birds, they are very tame and so wonderfully camouflaged that very often you nearly stumble over them before they take off with shrill cries, flying low over the water, showing a bold pied pattern. They almost always land again after a short flight so that you are able to see them at work. In small parties they delve among the weed and stones and debris, jerking it about and turning things over in the search for molluscs, insects and sand-hoppers. They are, in short, on the same job as you; they are honest beachcombers.

Very often parties of turnstones are accompanied by a small party of purple sandpipers. Rather portly birds, confiding and tame, they are easily missed but are especially fond of rocky places, weedy shores, weedy and encrusted piers and suchlike man-made structures, dodging the sea and chasing small morsels. Sanderlings are also very adept shore hunters; another plump wader, pale chestnut and white, not so much noticeable for their colour as for their extraordinary vitality. They steam along the edge of the surf like clockwork mice, snatching unfortunate bugs and worms from the very edge of the surf and the backwash.

At the uppermost limits of the shore live those animals that have almost made a break with the sea and learned to become land creatures. Chitons and sea slaters, with their woodlouse-like articulated armour-plates, scavenge during the night. Almost independent of the sea, they carry their eggs in a brood pouch, the young emerging in adult form without having enjoyed a larval stage as plankton animals. To gain access to the land, it is necessary for animals to be able to breathe air, to avoid desiccation, and to breed ashore without recourse to the sea. The chitons and sea slaters have gone a long way along this road, but the most fascinating demonstration of a family pioneering the route ashore is given by the periwinkles. There are four common species on the shore and each demonstrates a different stage in the process of invading the land. The common periwinkle is a very successful animal living over a wide area of the shore in large numbers. This is the creature harvested for food by winkle-pickers. Then there is the flat winkle, with its bladder-like appearance and tendency to disguise itself amongst the bladders of wrack. But the two smaller winkles of the upper shore are the ones of greatest interest in the pioneering stakes. The small periwinkle feeds mainly on lichens and is able to live high above the tideline provided it gets an occasional splash of sea water. Nonetheless, it still suffers the grave disadvantage of requiring a plankton stage for

HARD ROCK

The rock pipit is a common shore bird all the year round

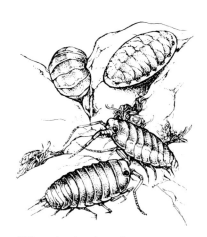

Chitons (top) and sea slaters

133

successful nurturing of its larvae.

The remaining species, the rough winkle, is an inhabitant of the upper shore, not venturing into the splash zone as adventurously as the small winkle. On the other hand it does have the all-important characteristic of being viviparous in its reproductive behaviour. The female produces live miniature snails, which are independent of the open sea plankton stage, and thus the species seems poised to make the final crawl up the beach to a life ashore. In fact this intertidal zone fringing the sea, so wonderfully rich in plants and animals, is a kind of transit camp, a place where creatures acclimatise themselves for the great change from life in the sea breathing water to life on the land breathing air, at first in short tidal gulps, then for longer periods higher up the shore, until they need only the occasional splash of salt spray to keep them going. And once they can crack the problem of producing young independently of the open sea, there is nothing to stop them forsaking the influence of salt water altogether. In a few million years' time, the common and inoffensive rough periwinkle of the seashore may be making its home in our fields and gardens, having passed through an evolutionary gateway.

7
Cliffs and Caves

Beachcombers may plod the sandy foreshore, but for distant horizons, and maybe a glimpse of some oceanic wanderer like a whale, there is nothing to beat the vantage point provided by a high cliff. When it stands squarely in the face of Atlantic storms, a cliff may be a raw and difficult habitat to colonise, but the plants and animals that live there will be correspondingly tough. Vertical cliff-faces, devoid of cracks and crevices, or cliffs formed of material so soft that it is continually weathering away, may be lifeless, but when wind, sea and weathering produce cracks and crannies, caves and ledges, then inevitably some hardy specimens take advantage of them.

Relatively few small birds are resident at the coast. The plump-headed stonechat is one of them, particularly well established in the coastal areas of Scotland, western Wales and the south and south-west of England. Severe winters in the past have reduced its numbers inland, but it is abundant along western coasts, nesting in heather and gorse, and feeding over rough ground, especially when there is some reed-fringed water nearby. If you walk the coastal paths in spring, you'll see its jaunty upright figure clinging high on stems, and insisting that you notice its alarm call – the clicking sound of pebbles being struck against each other.

A much rarer, or rather more localised, coastal bird is the cirl bunting. Rather   smaller   than   the   closely   related

135

yellowhammer, the male bird at least is easy enough to distinguish by its more strikingly marked head. And the song is a truncated version of the 'little-bit-of-bread-and-no-cheese', rattled away from the early spring right through until autumn. The species was first discovered to be breeding in Britain by a Colonel Montagu, of Kingsbridge in South Devon, in 1800, and its main stronghold is still the narrow coastal strip between Salcombe and Exeter, and National Trust properties like Bolberry Down, Little Dartmouth and Coleton Fishacre are promising locations to listen for it. The cirl bunting is best looked on as the Mediterranean form of the yellowhammer; its natural home is the hot terraced valleys of the vineyards. The gorsy clifftop walks of Devon represent the extreme northern limit of its range and its very existence here as a breeding bird depends upon mild winters.

The black redstart is another rare breeding species which showed some signs of establishing itself on the coast. On the continent it nests in mountain scree and on sea cliffs; range expansion first brought it to a tentative foothold in Sussex and Cornwall in the 1920s. Breeding sporadically in the south-east, it took unexpected advantage of the sudden increase in available nest sites in bomb-hit London in the 1940s. One of the more bizarre side effects of the conflict was the way in which these strikingly coloured birds began to establish themselves in the 'cliffsides' of bombed sites. There have been suggestions that their establishment in London was aided by the 'heat-island' effect which increases ambient temperature in big cities. Whatever the cause of their temporary success in London, the bomb sites are no longer available and black redstarts have turned instead to coastal versions of these industrial sites — places such as power stations. And they are now colonising the more typical coastal cliffs. Over the last three decades some thirty pairs have succeeded in breeding each year, but there is a long way to go before they are firmly established as British breeding birds.

Some members of the crow family have taken to coastal life and throughout the year they liven up any coastal excursion. The largest, and most splendid, is the raven. Wherever it can live without persecution, from the mountainous high tops by way of woodland to sea level, the raven may not be common but it is typically a bird of western Britain. Its hoarse resonant calls are unmistakable, and the large size and wedge-shaped tail help to identify this welcome bird — welcome to the land-based birdwatcher, anyway. Ravens, like certain other creatures — rabbits for instance — are traditionally beasts of ill-omen for sailors.

Ravens inhabit wild places, so the very sound and sight of them is a passport to wilderness. The largest of our crows, they have stout arched black bills and a purple-green gloss to their all-black plumage. With a 4ft (1.2m) wingspan, they soar high in the up-draughts and have superb aerobatic capability. Where they can breed in reasonable numbers they are gregarious birds, flocking together to feed on carrion and roosting sociably on cliffs, sometimes in parties of a hundred or more. Restless birds, they seem always to be on the move, swinging about the sky, landing for a short time on precipitous crags. One place where you can be almost certain of seeing them is at St Michael's Mount, the superb National Trust island property in Mount's Bay, West Cornwall, where, because of the shortage of suitably precipitous cliffs, ravens build their nest, uncharacteristically, in places where it is fairly easy to see them. They have three ancestral sites on the north-west face of the Mount, and tend to patronise a different one each year. Astonishing structures, the nests are massive and solid. Both members of the pair collect material, piling it onto the foundations that become larger and larger as the years go by. A seeming jumble of large sticks forms the core, then earth and turves prepare a bed for the relative comfort of the cup, which may be lined with sheep's wool and rabbit's fur. In Cornwall the birds will be renovating the nest site as early as January, when the young will be flying in May. A spring visit to St Michael's Mount will almost certainly be rewarded by some excellent raven-watching.

Jackdaws are very common around cliff sites. Although they take readily to town life when conditions favour them, they are equally at home on the wild open cliffs, foraging on the shore at low water and at all times on the open close-cropped sward of the cliff edge, in search of insects and seeds. There's no danger of mistaking them for ravens. Quite apart from their 'tchak' calls they are much smaller and generally quicker in their movements than their relatives. Given the chance, they will be quick to take advantage of other birds on cliff faces. If, for example, an auk should leave its egg unattended for a moment a jackdaw will move in for a feast. At one time it was considered possible that jackdaw predation was responsible for the general decline in auk numbers; on some islands jackdaws were shot in large numbers in an attempt to reverse the trend but the activity had little effect on the jackdaw population. Since the easy feeding on islands is attractive to jackdaws, the moment a vacant niche became available, new blood arrived from the mainland to maintain the numbers by immigration.

The other crow that is characteristic of the coastal habitat is the chough, the red-billed crow. Known in the Westcountry as the Cornish chough, it is sadly no longer present in the south-west at all, not having bred in Cornwall since the early 1940s. Nowadays this exciting bird is restricted to western Scotland, the north and west coast of Wales, the Isle of Man and Ireland. The reasons for its decline are not obvious, but once again the jackdaw cannot be blamed, for although the two close relatives share a habitat they are not in competition for nest sites or food. The choughs' downfall has perhaps been their over-specialised and un-crowlike feeding habits; they prefer the restricting diet of ants and 'ants' eggs' (actually the insects' pupae or larvae) for which they probe in the rabbit-cropped turf. Sociable birds, they wheel and turn in wild extravagant aerobatics above the sea, but it's almost easy to pass them by without noticing the curved red beak and spread wing tips that distinguish them from the all-pervasive jackdaws. The musical call 'cho' may well be the signal which draws your attention, and becomes immediately clear that their name is onomatopoeic, making a nonsense of the fact that nowadays we pronounce them 'chuff'.

Although in Wales choughs often nest far inland on quarry faces, the more typical nest site is high up in a sea cave or on an inaccessible ledge or crevice. The deer park peninsula of Martin's Haven, near Marloes, is as good a place as any to walk the cliff path in the hope of seeing a passing chough. Just as in the case of the raven, the nest is practically unreachable. It ought to be possible to attract choughs to artificial nest sites; in Ireland they have bred in disused lighthouses and in Martello towers and other derelict buildings.

The rock pipit is another resident bird that chooses to nest in cliff holes and crevices. Hunting for insects along the shoreline and amongst piles of rotting seaweed, they are birds of the upper shore. In spring the unremarkable looking male bird indulges in a charming display flight, where he leaps a few yards into the air in order to glide down, singing as he goes, to land on top of an outcrop. But at any time of the year these 'rockets' are anticipated companions on a walk along the rocky shore.

Small brown birds such as rock pipits don't fit the received image of longshore bird life, but shags and cormorants, which are widespread around our coast, are surely everyone's idea of coastal species. Though they appear superficially similar it is fairly easy to become adept at distinguishing the two birds. Cormorants are larger, standing a good couple of inches – some

5cm – higher. In the breeding season their glossy black plumage sports a white patch on either side behind the wing, and they always show a white face and chin patch. Shags have a rather more snake-like head and neck, and their plumage has more of an oily greenish tinge. At one time they were commonly called green cormorants. In the breeding season they have a distinct quiff to their heads, in which the feathers form a forward-curving crest.

When it is time to breed, both cormorants and shags frequent inshore rocks and islands, enjoying the freedom from disturbance offered by coastal 'mewstones'. Both are colonial by preference, but whereas cormorants nest close together and in the open, shags choose rather more private ledges and dark crevices, and are more loosely associated with their kind. The nests of both species are quite elaborate, with seaweeds and various trifles picked from the surface of the sea forming a cup-lining inside a bulky base of twigs. Throughout the incubation period and even when the chicks are near to leaving the nest, the parents persist in decorating and improving the happy home, weaving plastic beach toys and other bric-à-brac around the rim of the cup.

Cormorants lay three or four bluish-white eggs and the parents share the duties of incubation for a month. Unusually for birds, they have no bare brood patch with which to warm the eggs, but their blood system provides for a rich supply to their feet. So the cormorant actually stands on its eggs, covering them with its warm paddles, before settling to incubate. The young are born blind and naked, and remarkably reptilian in aspect, but soon grow a dense black down that sheds as the juvenile plumage appears. A couple of times a day they're fed with a rich and thick soup of well digested fish, which is regurgitated by the parent in response to the purposeful exploration of its gullet by the juvenile. They become independent at about ten weeks of age.

At one time cormorants were severely persecuted by ignorant fishermen, in the mistaken belief that they caused harm to fish stocks simply by being more efficient than the anglers in pursuit of fish. Even water authorities, which ought to know better but sometimes don't, used to offer rewards in exchange for dead cormorants. Of course, cormorants can do a lot of damage in a stewpond where a superabundance of fish is kept in unnatural conditions, but in the normal course of events in natural conditions they act simply as predators, carrying out their allotted tasks of regulating animal numbers.

Both cormorants and shags are resident birds, remaining

Top In courtship plumage, the cormorant has a white throat and thigh patches, while the shag sports a crest; *bottom* the cormorant (right) is larger and heavier-necked, the shag having a more elegant snake-like neck; if in doubt, count the tail feathers – cormorants have fourteen, shags twelve within a fairly short distance of their birthplace. Coastal plants could be said to display much the same fidelity, but, like the birds, they are merely well adapted to their habitat and way of life. Plants can't move, except in the sense that they can explore and colonise by means of their seeds. And coastal plants are by nature tough, designed to cope with a testing variety of conditions and sites. Exposed cliff faces may be unsympathetic places for plants to establish themselves, but the weathering processes of wind, rain and frost eventually produce cracks and crannies and debris enough to offer a foothold. It is in the lower levels, where tolerance of salt spray is mandatory, that maritime plants are seen at their hardiest. It is only the specialists that exist in these harsh conditions. They tend to be perennials, wind and salt hardened by an environment that favours maturity and discourages brash youth. The hopeful seed imported by the temporary visit of a bird to a crevice has all the odds stacked against it. Even if there is enough soil in the crevice to support germination, there is every chance of being blown away by the wind or of suffering a lethal drying out in the hot sun. But if it can establish a toe-hold, then its very presence acts as a wind break, allowing more soil-forming detritus to pile up in the crevice, thus giving the youthful plant more of a chance. As it grows, its roots will probe deeply in the search for moisture and, growing woody and fibrous, they will serve as an anchor.

Exposure to a succession of gales reduces the range of competition amongst cliff plants. Unless there is a fair degree of shelter there will be few trees along the coast. Monterey pines were introduced to Britain from California in the 1830s with the object of providing coastal shelter belts. On the eastern side of the entrance to Dartmouth harbour, for instance, there is a most attractive stand of these trees. Impressively large, they display a dense foliage of vivid emerald green needles. The pines' rapid growth, as much as three feet (nearly a metre) a year, has made them useful for the timber trade in Australia and New Zealand, but they provide a rather coarse product, which is regarded as non-commercial in Britain. But in the milder parts, for instance in the south-west, they serve well in their role of decorative shelter belt.

If a plant can tolerate the awkward gradients and soil sparsity of a cliff, it is able to benefit from the lack of competition. Where rabbits and sheep cannot graze plants may flourish, but different plants flourish in clearly defined zones which relate to their tolerance to the presence of salt sea-water. In the areas below the higher reach of the big spring tides, you are in the region of the seaweeds, whose many forms are dictated by the duration of tidal submersion; from the air- and sun-tolerant green weeds of the upper zone by way of the medium-sized mid-shore brown wracks to the monstrous low-water kelps and the totally submerged red weeds. Above the reach of the tide, but within the sphere of influence of the salt-water spray, the 'splash zone' is characterised by the hardy lichens. Then come the ledge and crevice plants that are able to withstand a modicum of salt spray, and are thereby described as *halophytes*. Our only maritime fern, sea spleenwort, is one of these, a plant that hides itself in shady cracks on the cliffs of the west coast. Perhaps thrift is the best known and loved of these salt-tolerant plants. The dry and windy conditions of cliff faces and slopes are too exacting for most plants, and thrift thrives in spite of the salt rather than because of it.

Some of the cliffside plants are surprisingly large and impressive. The vigorous tree mallow grows practically to the height of a man's chest. With its large pink flowers, it is abundant in the far west of Devon and Cornwall at places like Berry Head, near Brixham, for instance. Often you will find it in profusion on the outskirts of sea-bird colonies, where it proves its ability to survive high levels of nitrogen and phosphorus, deposited as droppings by the roosting and socialising birds. Another astonishing plant, which sometimes threatens to take over the steep cliffsides in the Westcountry, is the Hottentot fig or ice-plant, *Carpobrotus edulis*, which has fleshy leaves and large yellow flowers. Originally introduced from South Africa as a garden plant, it has spread to establish itself in abundance. In the Isles of Scilly it was used, experimentally, along with marram grass, to stabilise sand dunes. Once it has a foothold it increases to cover large areas in a short time, successfully ousting the native plants. Indeed, in Scilly, the ice-plant is now well established all over the place, spread partly by man but also by the activities of the gulls which use pieces of the plant for their nests, thus affording an opportunity for yet more spread.

Almost as spectacular as the ice-plant in late spring are the massed yellow flowers and large blue-green leaves of the wild cabbage which spreads abundantly over steep cliff slopes. Like sea-beet and sea-kale, the wild cabbage provided the stock for our cultivated varieties. Indeed many of our most important food plants have their ancestral roots back on the sea coast. Sea-beet grows freely on shingle and on strandlines, as well as on the cliffs, and flourishes with the help of a certain amount of bird droppings. A coarse perennial with fleshy roots, it straggles

Sea-beet, a tough perennial which grows well on sand and shingle as well as on sea cliffs

Rock samphire, a maritime plant confined to sea cliffs, quay walls and embankments

over the ground producing a delicious profusion of leaves. The younger ones taste excellent prepared as spinach, and indeed garden spinach is a cultivated form. At one time its close relative, sea-kale, was grown extensively in Britain, but nowadays it is an uncommon vegetable. In times past people would blanch it *in situ* by covering the wild crowns with a foot or so of shingle.

There are other cliff plants with culinary value. Leaves of fennel are used for salad dressings and in fish sauces and soups. Oil extracted from the aromatic fruits has various uses for condiment manufacturers and confectioners, and the fruits are listed in the British Pharmaceutical Codex as a cure for flatulence! The most famous of the edible plants is rock samphire, a tender green stalk some 2ft – 60cm – high, branching out into numbers of thick round leaves. The white flowers, in July and August, are followed by seeds something like those of fennel. The root is very large and white. The plant grows on and above the spray zone on rocky cliffs, and also on sand and shingle. Both leaves and root have a hot spicy taste, and at one time they were much used for making pickle. 'Crest marine' was the cry in London streets. William Borlase, writing of the natural history of Cornwall in the eighteenth century, said 'Among the rock and cliff-plants the Samphire may be reckoned the most useful. Some boil it as a pot-herb; picked, it is thought to help digestion: Dr Leigh thinks it may be ranked in the first class of antiscorbutics.' It also has a rich iodine content. In Culpeper's *Herbal*, he adjures us all to take it as a remedy for the 'ill digestions and obstructions [which] are the cause of most of the diseases which the frail nature of man is subject to'. Shakespeare has the hard-pressed King Lear look over the cliff to where 'half-way down hangs one that gathers samphire, dreadful trade'.

Red campion is a nitrogen-loving plant that benefits from the droppings of sea-birds, becoming especially prolific in those areas where lesser black-backed gulls have their nesting and courting grounds. Its luscious pink flowers are also typical of the slopes below gannet and puffin colonies, provided there's not too much wind-blown salt spray. Rabbits don't much like red campion, only eating it as a penance, another factor that encourages its growth. White sea-campion is a close relative, but more typical of warmer, drier climates and at the edge of its distribution range in Britain.

Once above or back from the ravages of salt spray, the plants of the cliff are less specialised. Grasses, such as red fescue, become commonplace, and stonecrop does well. As the gradients become less extreme you enter the regions grazed by rabbits, sheep and cattle. Indeed towards the top of a cliff the plant community becomes that typical of heath or scrubland. Back from the edge and out of the teeth of salt-laden winds heather and gorse begin to show their faces; there is altogether a greater profusion of species. The winds that are characteristic of cliff life make conditions unfavourable for flying insects, and the fauna tends to be recognisably terrestrial, grasshoppers, snails and woodlice predominating. This is the kind of coastal habitat favouring the occasional family of badgers, which enjoys a well-drained sunny aspect, relatively undisturbed and well supplied with worms.

Cliff birds are best seen from the top of the cliff, against a background of heaving sea. While the gulls are haunting the rubbish tips and begging for handouts on the promenade, the true sea-going birds may show themselves, in passing, to the patient cliff-top watcher. Choose a place where the coast points a finger well out into the sea – a promontory, or perhaps the furthermost horn of a bay. The best seawatching places are those where passage birds are 'turning a corner' from one patch of sea to another, and where they are closest to land. From a good vantage point you may see distant gannets, whiter-than-white, or large parties of auks or shearwaters on migration. Although you will be lucky to see an albatross, very much a chance visitor, there is a strong likelihood of seeing a close relative – the fulmar – almost anywhere around the coast of Britain. Sit patiently at the top of a rugged cliff, and sooner or later a bold gull-like bird will soar around the corner, pass close to you with direct stare, then glide away, perhaps to reappear a

CLIFFS AND CAVES

A fine vantage point for watching cliff birds

143

Fulmar in flight

Fulmar chicks repel intruders with a jet of fish-oil

short while later to repeat the performance. The more you see of it, the clearer it becomes that it is not a gull at all. The soaring flight, the thick-necked, rather stocky appearance, and the narrow, stiffly outstretched wings, reveal the bird as a petrel, not to be written off as a 'seagull'.

Fulmars have been well established in this country for many centuries, but until relatively recently they were confined to remote islands like Foula in Shetland and the Hebridean St Kilda. Over the last two hundred years, however, they have expanded their range in the most astonishing demonstration of ornithological colonisation. Nowadays, although their presence is weakest in the south-east, they nest on almost any suitable cliff in the British Isles. A bare, wind-blown ledge serves their purpose for breeding, and the single white egg is incubated without the benefit of any warmly-lined nest cup. There is no attempt at nest concealment, since the fulmar chick, which spends a good deal of time alone, has an effective and disconcerting method of discouraging intruders. Faced with an unwelcome visitor, the young bird spouts a stinking jet of fish oil through its beak, reaching a surprising distance and with surprising accuracy.

Fulmars are doing well, but not for the same reasons as gulls. They do not resort to sewage farms and fish quays; instead they benefit greatly from man's activities far out at sea. Although the precise reasons for the success of the fulmar are not universally agreed, it seems likely that the species has gained advantage from the formidable growth first in whaling and then in trawling. These industries involve the processing of fish at sea, with a consequent bonanza of offal for the scavengers. The significant warming of the north Atlantic towards the latter part of the last century may also be a factor in their population increase. Whatever the reason, our coasts are now much enriched by the pleasurable sight of fulmars soaring and wheeling.

In the breeding season peregrines are typically falcons of the sea cliffs, nesting on ledges or in holes, at sites that may have been continuously occupied right back to medieval times. Perching on a rocky pinnacle, with head sunk menacingly between its shoulders, the peregrine is king of the cliffs. Fast flying machines, with pointed wings and a tapering tail, they dash about the cliff faces, keeping a weather eye open for food. Although it is true they will take a rabbit on occasion, their primary prey is seabirds and pigeons. Once decided upon, the prey, itself on the wing, is taken in flight, the peregrine swooping down with folded wings at great speed, perhaps as much as 200mph (320kmph), and breaking the neck of the prey. Then, taking the carcass back to its rocky pinnacle, it plucks it at leisure.

While the homing pigeon, crossing the coast on racing passage back to an inland loft, is certainly in danger from peregrines, in historical times the falcon would traditionally have preyed on the more purely coastal wild rock dove, as well as on stock doves visiting cliff tops to forage. Nowadays the rock dove is, sadly, a decreasing species, surviving only on remote coasts and islands in Scotland and Ireland. Rock doves are perfectly at home in these wild places, and their swift and daring flight has something of the verve of the peregrine about it, although it may not be as fast as the falcon. Striking birds, rock doves have the two distinct black wing bars and whitish rump which are so often seen on the common street pigeons which live so comfortably in our cities. The connection between the two is very close and is intimately bound up with man's progress in agriculture.

Many hundreds of years ago, preserving enough food to get through the winter was much more of a problem than it is now. Few farmers could store enough hay to maintain more than a small breeding nucleus of cattle, sheep and pigs, and refrigeration was the prerogative of the very few who could afford an ice house. For most people, salted meat was the rule and fresh meat the rare exception. Rock doves, which could almost have been designed for domestication, provided the answer. Placid, with undemanding breeding requirements, their strong suit was a natural inclination to produce fat young (squabs) at all seasons of the year, because of their ability to rear their young on pigeon 'milk'. With careful management, they could be used to provide fresh meat until the spring and summer came again. Rock doves breed in caves, and it was very soon realised that by providing extra ledges, more nests (and thus more squabs) would be produced. Before long, it was also realised that it would save a lot of trouble if the birds were brought to artificial caves inland, in order to spread the delights of pigeon pie to those whose residences were far from the roar of the sea. Thus, dovecotes became established, and highly successful they were, providing fresh winter meat through the centuries until eighteenth-century man discovered the potential of root crops and so cracked the problem of feeding domestic animals through the year.

Today these old pigeon houses stand idle, but the descendants of their occupants are still going strong, as street pigeons and homers. Not infrequently racing pigeons drop out

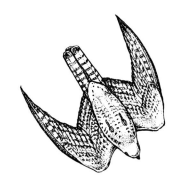

The peregrine falcon dives at a speed of up to 200mph (320kph) when attacking a pigeon or other prey

Rock doves are very rare nowadays but feral pigeons, their direct descendants, often take their place

145

A dovecote

of the race and retire to live on the coast. The result is that though pure rock doves may be confined to the far north and west, these impure pigeons whose remote ancestors lived on the coasts of Britain now carry on the tradition. Feral pigeons are very common all round our coastline, living as their ancestors did, breeding in caves and foraging for seeds on the cliff tops. Although the first generation of cliff colonists may wear a racing ring, their progeny do not, and the cliffs and bays echo to the whirr and clap of the wings of flocks of pigeons that are as wild as anyone might reasonably wish. Now that the peregrine population is recovering, though, they are likely to flourish less freely.

Apart from the rare choughs and the common pigeons, the other noteworthy inhabitant of sea caves is the grey seal. Choosing the remotest and most isolated breeding sites on islands and storm-racked sections of the mainland, the superb grey seal is an animal totally at home in these places of fierce currents and white-water overfalls. Much persecuted in the past, seals now enjoy a certain measure of legal protection and a full measure of popular sympathy, though there is a running battle between them and the commercial fishermen, who have the usual fisherman's objection to anything which competes for their prey.

In Britain we are privileged to play host to about half the world population of grey seals, which are rare in world terms, so it behoves us to take good care of them. While it is perfectly true that grey seals have increased their numbers spectacularly since protection began, the quantity of fish they take is insignificant, compared with the annual catch of the fishing industry. It is to be hoped that long-term management plans for control of seal populations will take the welfare of the seals as their main consideration, leaving fishermen to continue

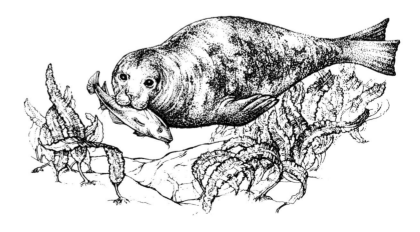

Grey seal fishing

enjoying the lion's share of the fish stocks.

Grey seals are sociable animals, gathering close together in large numbers, sometimes several hundreds at a time, for assemblies before and after the breeding season. On the breeding beaches, however, they tend to keep a certain distance from their fellows, and the bull seals do not come ashore at all. Choosing the remotest beach or inaccessible cave, the cow seal hauls herself up, often above high water mark, to drop her pup. It is important that even at high water of spring tides there is a strand of dry beach for the pup to rest on. If the place is well chosen and undisturbed, the new-born animal may lie still, almost motionless except at feeding time, for the whole first month of its life. Often enough, though, it will go down to the water and swim about a while and then join its mother to suckle contentedly from the breast as she lies at the tide's edge.

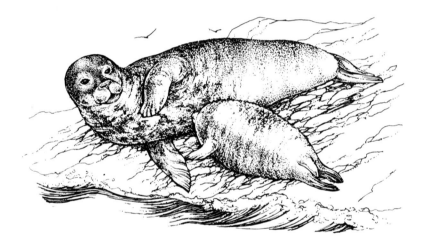

Grey seal with pup feeding

Though the pup's coat is yellowish-cream at birth, the hair soon becomes white, and after a couple of weeks of rich feeding its body assumes the shape of a barrel and it begins to moult into its sea-going coat. As the grey pelage begins to appear at the head, muzzle and flippers, discarded white hairs mount up on the pebbles around the recumbent body. From a birth weight of perhaps 33lb (15kg), the healthy animal will have grown to about 110 lb (50kg) a month later when, bloated with blubber, it is abandoned by its mother and, hungry, must find its own way to sea and learn to fish.

It is in their first few weeks at sea, in early winter, that young seals very often encounter storms and come ashore exhausted. Like those young shelducklings, it is in this condition that well meaning rescuers either take the animals home with them, or try to launch them into the sea again, believing mistakenly that they cannot survive out of water. All they need is a little peace and quiet so that they can revive. Then, when the time is ripe, they will go off again.

These babies, which are invariably described in press reports as abandoned, are only rarely in need of food. If you have reason to believe that the seal is in genuine distress, then it can be fed either by stomach tube or by force feeding raw fish. If it is new-born or only a few days old, still in its white coat, then use a liquid mixture of 50 per cent agricultural fish meal and 50 per cent baby milk, with added cod liver oil. Ease a greased tube down through its mouth and into its stomach. Attach a funnel to the top and pour a pint or so of the mixture in in one fell swoop. The youngster can take more than you expect, and three times a day. If it is lively enough to bite and plunge about, you will need an assistant to straddle the animal and hold its mouth open with heavy gloves. If it is this lively then it can digest raw fish, which you will probably have to force down its throat with a stick. But please remember that the *likely* thing is that the seal is looking only for a rest, and get qualified advice if you possibly can. A sick or injured seal should, of course, be attended by a veterinary surgeon. And it is your job to pay the bill!

But if all goes well and the young seal avoids 'rescue' and makes its own way to sea, in its first year of life it will travel, perhaps many hundreds of miles – a Welsh pup may visit France, and a Scottish or Northumberland pup may visit Norway – but in due course, if all goes well, it will return to the home beach or cave, and probably spend the rest of its life enjoying the wild seashore.

Other mammals that you may see from the cliffs are porpoises, dolphins and whales. On occasion quite large numbers of porpoises and dolphins may come close inshore to take advantage of a shoal of mackerel or mullet. Mostly all you will see is the dorsal fin rolling over and reappearing in slow rhythm. Very occasionally one of them may leap right out into the open and hang suspended before falling back with a mighty splash. Killer whales and pilot whales are sometimes seen around our coasts, but on the whole the chance of seeing them is small, and the chance of being eaten by one is even smaller.

The largest animal you are likely to see inshore is the second biggest fish in the world, the basking shark. Averaging some 20ft (6m) in length, they cruise slowly along, just under the surface and sometimes very close inshore, with their wide-open mouths gulping in the plankton. They are easily distinguished from the whales by the fact that the large dorsal fin and tail fin are showing above water most of the time, whereas the whales' fins appear and disappear regularly in time with their breathing pattern. The great fish has no need to come to the surface to breathe, of course, and he just continues to suck up plankton in a phlegmatic manner. Although the appearance of a basking shark is guaranteed to clear the sea of bathers, the fact is that they quite harmless. The only danger is that if you swim too close he may panic and, in diving, scrape your skin off with his sharkskin or knock you out with his flailing tail.

Harmless they may be, like most sharks, but like the wolf and the fox, they bear the wrong name and have to carry the can for centuries of ignorant character-blacking. Fortunately for them, the baskers are plankton feeders and will not take bait, or they would doubtless become the quarry of sport fishermen, and yet another virility symbol would be born. Other sharks, being honest predators, are more vulnerable. Even in this enlightened age, people become heroes by virtue of catching a shark, a feat requiring no skill but a strong stomach and a certain amount of brute force.

Baskers appear off the west coasts of Scotland and Ireland in April/May and off the south-west around about June, when they are in evidence for only a few weeks. At one time they were hunted for their valuable liver oil, a fairly dangerous occupation, but nowadays they are mostly left alone on their majestic cruise of the shoreline.

8

Islands

Islands may be only pieces of land surrounded by water, but they have an interest and value out of all proportion to their physical size. Thousands of them exist, yet new ones are constantly being formed. A new island gives cause for rejoicing, whether it is a brand new world thrust hissing and bubbling through the sea by a volcano, giving man a chance to extend his territorial waters and stake new claims; a sheer rock at last separated from its parent cliff; or an ephemeral island, appearing only when the tide drops, to provide a convenient resting place for our coastal birds or seals.

Some nine thousand years ago Britain became an island. Not a dramatic event, it took place gradually over a few thousand years, during the waning of the last Ice Age, long enough for plants and animals and people to decide which side of the water they were going to live. During the Ice Age, great continental ice-sheets clothed the land. All that frozen water, locked up on the land, had come from the ocean and had the direct effect of lowering the level of the sea in relation to the land. But the Ice Age was not uniformly cold. There were warmer interludes, when glaciers began to melt, returning some water to the sea. Then there were colder periods, again with more ice, so the sea level went up and down in sympathy. Eventually, the shift to a warmer and wetter climate became more permanent. The ice, which had clothed the whole of Britain north of a line drawn roughly between the Severn and the Thames, began to melt, bringing the sea and its influence higher on to the land, until finally the last of the dry land, where ships now sail the Straits of Dover, was submerged. That probably happened about 5500BC.

We became an island race because the rising sea cut us off from the rest of Europe. But there are other ways of island-building, and they are going on all the time around the shores of Britain. Take, for example, the formation of mud banks, which is particularly common in the south-east of England. This comes about because the sea level is still rising – about $^1/_{25}$in – 1mm – a year is the current estimate. The rise in level means that rivers flow more sluggishly, because they are gradually being robbed of their downhill gradient to the sea. Slower waters have less energy to carry their burdens of mud and silt, so they drop them, to form mud banks, which gradually increase in size and height until they achieve the status of dry land.

Another kind of low-lying island, close to the shore, can be formed when off-shore sand and shingle banks grow sufficiently to raise their heads above the waves at all states of the tide. Walney Island, famous for its breeding birds, probably came about in this way, and in January 1972 the British Isles increased their number by yet one more, when a new island appeared off the Isle of Wight, a mile north-west of the Needles. As the coastguards explained to *The Times*, 'There has been a shingle bank there for years, but it must have built up, and is now three or four feet out of the water'.

The famous Needles of the Isle of Wight are islands themselves, of course, but were formed in a very different way. They were the result of erosion – chips off the old block. The erosive power of sea waves seeks out weaknesses in the cliffs and exploits them relentlessly. Given time, a crack becomes a chasm, and in yet more time the sea may rush through. The jointing pattern in the chalk at the western end of the Isle of Wight has thus determined the existence of the islands or 'stacks' of the Needles. Many islands that lie close to the shore are formed in this way. Favourite resting places for birds, they give an extra dimension to the coastline. They are the result of differential erosion, and above all other factors it is their geology which ordained that they would become islands.

The powerful appeal of islands is easy to understand, whether it is to own one, to live on one, or merely to visit one to camp, play, and pretend to be pirates. People are fascinated by islands and often give them a notoriety out of all proportion to their size. Small islands tend to be inhabited by recluses, scientists, eccentrics and poets, but if they are big enough, they grow to support specialised versions of mainland society. The Isles of Scilly, the Isle of Wight and the Isle of Man are good examples. On an island, the human communities are different

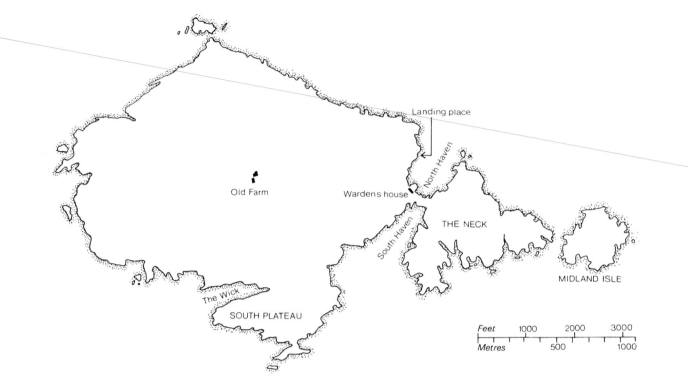

Skomer island and the 'Neck' – an island of the future?

to those of the mainland. Their problems, such as communications, building sites and shelter, have always forced them to be so. And it is the same for the plants and animals. So while many things on an island may be the same as the mainland – the rock, the soil, the climate – the factor that makes all the difference is the separation.

Skomer, off the southern horn of St Bride's Bay, is separated from the Pembrokeshire coast by a mere thousand yards – 915m. The main mass of the island, 722 acres (292ha) of it, is made of strong igneous rock, resisting for the most part the attack of the sea. In some places, however, where softer sedimentary rocks meet the sea, the result of their weakness can be seen. The 'Neck' is the best place to look, for here the sea to the north and south of the island is divided in one place by only 36ft (11m) of land – a defence that is being gradually whittled away by a sea intent on forming yet another new island. In this way Middleholm was cut off from Skomer, and the forces which managed to do this can well be imagined by watching Jack Sound when the tide is running.

With a westerly gale to help it, the flooding tide may drive a furious seven knot current, forcing a maelstrom of white water through the narrow gap between Middleholm and the mainland. And the even narrower gap between Middleholm and Skomer is hardly less wild. The eddies and overfalls caused by numerous isolated rocks confuse the scene and the violent tide-race strikes awe into the heart of any sailor. Yet, in reasonable weather and with local knowledge, the Sounds are navigable and the passage to Skomer is a peaceful and pleasureable half-hour trip. In the summer months the boat will make its way across a sea alive with puffins and guillemots, razorbills and fulmars. Long before the wide-open arms of North Haven welcome you to the island itself, you are warming to the magic of the place. Steep cliffs guard a central plateau, a tableland some 200ft (60m) above sea level, and the whole land mass is a natural sanctuary for wild creatures, including people, protected from the fierce competition of the mainland. There is security here, where seabirds may nest safe from attack by mainland predators such as foxes and stoats. The climate is mild, with less rain than in other parts of West Wales, and whilst the weather may be changeable, gales and rainstorms are usually mercifully brief, and frost is almost unknown.

Skomer has been inhabited for a long time. Although there is no documentary evidence pre-dating the Norman occupation, there is plenty of visible proof that people have lived there since at least the Iron Age. Below the rocky outcrops leading to the Mewstone are the clear outlines of field enclosures, with the hut sites and circles of a community that lived over 2,000 years ago. Those long-dead farmers must have found it worthwhile to brave the crossing, and there is no reason to suppose that they lived anything but a full life. With plenty of rich grazing for goats, cattle and sheep, they occupied an island that was easy to defend and lacked the wolves and beasts of prey, which must have been common on the mainland. In addition to their domestic stock, they enjoyed a summer influx of seabirds, which must have improved their living standards enormously. It has been calculated that they could have had the pick of a hundred thousand fresh eggs and, later, 70,000 fat young birds – representing some twenty-five tons of edible meat. With fresh meat in summer and dried in winter, they need have suffered no shortage, though doubtless they complained of a monotonous diet.

Today the island, owned by the Nature Conservancy Council and managed by the West Wales Naturalists' Trust, is inhabited only in summer. The warden and his family live there, visited by working scientists and large numbers of day trippers anxious to sample the richness of the wildlife. Although conditions are by no means luxurious, at least the scientists have the benefit of a well built timber house, something that

Fulmar at the nest site

153

Buzzard at nest in cliff crevice

On treeless islands, crows may build in bramble bushes

the early settlers would have found very difficult to construct, for one of the significant omissions from the island's plant list is trees. There are precious few of them, finding what shelter they can from the salt-laden Atlantic gales. Yet even in the absence of trees, tree-nesting predators like buzzards and crows maintain a healthy presence. Forsaking their natural preferences, the buzzards build nest mounds in sheltered rock crevices overlooking the sea, and the crows make do with what they can find, nesting in bramble clumps, and old field walls.

Skomer makes up for its lack of trees with a rich carpet of other plants. There is, after all, a diversity of habitats here, from the freshwater lake in the centre of the high plateau, through acres of good grazing and gentle slopes to the steep cliffs at the sea's edge. Landing on the island in June, a first impression is of a vast carpet of red, white and blue, where the strong colour of red campion, and the white flowers of sea campion growing thickly on the cliff slopes, contrast with the fast-fading bluebells. And as you plod up the grassy cliff path, it becomes clear that the bluebells are associated with the most extensive plant of all — bracken. In the face of cool Atlantic winds its crozier shoots are slow to unfold, but as the days go by, it dominates the island flora. The lesser celandines and ground ivy, which live cheek by jowl with the bracken, will already have flowered and seeded in the spring sunshine. Other plants benefit from the developing bracken — wood sage, Yorkshire fog and the fescue grasses all do well in the damp shady area under its umbrella. But the bluebell is the plant that benefits most of all from its presence. Close to its protector, the blooms are thickest. Normally a woodland plant, it enjoys the moisture conserved by the sun-sheltering fronds of bracken.

Bracken cannot survive in the face of the severe winds and on the thin soil of the exposed south-west part of the island. In these areas, the most spectacular plant show is provided by cushion-beds of thrift, which grows so extensively in some parts that you have no choice but to walk on it and enjoy the spring it puts in your step. On a warm day it makes one of the more memorable resting-places of anyone's life.

Away from the sea campion and thrift slopes, the plants in the most exposed areas exhibit the classic outcome of selective suppression by wind and grazing. Both influences produce similar effects, favouring the growth of dwarf forms that hug the surface of the ground, hardly showing their faces. But the most powerful influence of all is that of rabbits, which impose a rigorous grazing test on any plant wanting to survive. From the casual visitor's point of view, the close cropped springy pasture is one of the delights of the island, but a superabundance of rabbits certainly results in a less luxurious plant cover. Rather in the way that one of the few garden lawn plants which can survive repeated close shaves with a lawnmower is the dandelion, so the rabbit infested areas on Skomer are characterised by hardy ground-hugging, rosette plants.

Rabbits were brought to islands by farmers in search of an honest profit. While rabbit warrens were first established on the mainland in the Middle Ages, the species could have been designed for islands, with their lack of ground predators. Rabbit meat and rabbit skins were long regarded as luxuries, fetching a high price. In 1324 the Earl of Pembroke held the rights to Skomer Island. At that time the pasturage was valued at £2.75, the annual return from rabbits was £14.25. So a pattern of farming was established. Through the winter ferreters worked the warrens. In spring sea-bird eggs and, later, the fat chicks were collected. Then the grazing was enjoyed by summering cattle and sheep. Arable farmers arrived around 1700, building a farmhouse and exporting high quality seed corn. The Skomer farm flourished until the mid-twentieth century, when labour and transport problems brought it to an end.

Through the centuries, times without number the warreners' rabbits have escaped, to set up feral populations and increase mightily. It seems incredible today to consider that at the turn of the twelfth century the tenant of Lundy was permitted, by privilege, only to take 50 rabbits in one year.

In 1955 myxomatosis wiped out the major part of all rabbit populations in the islands, as on the mainland, but the inevitable recovery took place and, while the disease is well established, rabbits have come to terms with it. On some remote islands black rabbits, selectively bred for their fur value in ornamental trimming, can still be seen.

The influence of the rabbit on island pasture is clear — continuous nibbling produces a close-cropped turf which is springy and pleasant to walk over. The constant cropping encourages the spread of ground-hugging plant forms. Because rabbits enjoy grasses, sea-pinks have room to flourish and decorate the cliff slopes. In fact the cliffside vegetation is held in equilibrium by their activities. However, it is true to say that where there are no rabbits there is a more luxuriant growth of more species of plants.

With the exception of seals and, in the far north, otters, most mammals have found their way to Britain's offshore islands as a consequence of human activity. In prehistoric times, men brought sheep and cattle to islands to take advantage of the

Thrift, the universal seaside plant, equally at home on cliff-top turf, saltmarsh or stable shingle; well able to change its shape to suit the environment, the plant may grow in flattened rosette form on exposed cliffs (or mountain tops where it also flourishes), or develop thick cushions of luxuriant leaves where the climate is kinder

summer grazing — at the same time helping themselves from the abundant supplies of birds and eggs. More recently, the export of island-fattened livestock has flourished because of the prime quality of the animals. The problems have always been those of transport and wintering.

In the St Kilda group, there have been Soay sheep for at least a thousand years, their ancestry directly relating to the Neolithic root-stock of domestication. Small, goat-like and dark chocolate-brown in colour, they are the most primitive of breeds, but they are able to endure the harsh winter without assistance. They owe their survival in such unchanged form to the benefits of island isolation — no fresh blood disturbing their genetic flow. Soays may also be seen in Ailsa Craig and Lundy, and there is a thriving flock on Cardigan Island, although the animals that were introduced to the Pembrokeshire islands of Skokholm and Skomer no longer exist. I remember the wild frustration of trying to capture these sheep on Skokholm, when Ronald Lockley wanted to establish a flock at his embryo Field Centre at Orielton. However we tried, there was no way to herd them; they dashed in all directions and then found sanctuary on impossible cliff ledges. Unlike the currently fashionable domestic breeds, these Soays are very much at home on fearsome cliff-slopes.

On North Ronaldsay, the most northerly of the Orkneys, is a breed of small short-tailed sheep that lives largely on seaweed, their meat being dark and rich with iodine. Under the auspices of the Rare Breeds Survival Trust, a flock nucleus was shipped to the tidal island of Lihou, off Guernsey, some years ago. They flourished on a diet consisting of one third grass and two thirds seaweed and now there are about a hundred of them. Every day, as the tide drops back, the sheep pick their way over the slippery boulders to graze the rich meadows of wrack and kelp.

Goats have wrought more havoc to the islands of the world than it is possible to imagine. Released by generations of island colonisers or passing mariners to multiply and provide milk and flesh on demand, they have taken to the feral life with gusto, reducing many a paradise to a barren slum. It might have been better for us all if these creatures, first domesticated thousands of years ago, had been left undisturbed in their rocky fastnesses in the far corners of Europe and Asia. But apart from their usefulness as a provider of milk, they have served sheep farmers in a curious manner. By eating the choicer grass, which is to be found on the most awkward cliff ledges, they reduce the incentive for the less agile sheep to try to emulate them — thus reducing the shepherd's losses.

On Lundy, in the Bristol Channel, feral goats were abundant, but the last survivors of a large herd of white goats were killed in the late nineteenth century. The Trinity House lighthouse keepers re-introduced them, for milk, in the late twenties. As on so many previous occasions on numberless other islands, some individuals soon escaped. At one time there was a wild population of some 200, though there are fewer today.

Broadly speaking, the same is true of red deer. Once ranging the greater part of Europe, they have been progressively exterminated by the destruction of their forest habitat and, on islands, by persecution. In the nineteenth century they were re-introduced to the Scottish islands in the name of sport. As the years go by, the scramble for prize 'heads' has been overtaken by the more logical and ecologically acceptable concept of management, where the annual cull, though it may well be exercised by sportsmen paying large fees for the privilege, is nevertheless aimed at maintaining a healthy population. The victims are selected not for the excellence of their antlers but in order to leave behind a balance of age groups representing the healthiest stock. So the yearly harvest leaves the herd in good shape. On the island of Rhum, in the Inner Hebrides, the re-introduced red deer are farmed by the scientists of the Nature Conservancy, whose object is to study the biology and management of the species. Though the native stock was exterminated in the eighteenth century, there are some 1,500 of these magnificent beasts on the island today.

As part of the management programme the island also supports a couple of dozen Rhum ponies which serve as pack animals to bring in the deer carcasses from the hills. These small horses, never higher than 14 hands, are the product of Arab sire and West Highland mares. Kept free of Clydesdale or similar heavy horse blood, they are typical of the saddle and pack animals that serve remote island communities. Big enough to do the required work, they have small appetites, fending for themselves throughout the year, though mares in foal, and foals and yearlings get some extra feed. The Shetland pony is a triumph of selective breeding, less than 11 hands high, by comparison with the Shire horse's 17. But the Icelandic pony is the typical form of light Celtic horse, one of several sub-species deriving from the original pre-historic European stock. Good load carriers but frugal eaters, some of them can subsist to a certain extent on a seaweed diet.

While the sheep, goats, cattle and rabbits were brought intentionally to islands by colonising man, other less welcome mammals arrived unintentionally. The mainland wood mouse, shrews and the brown rat were transported along with the fodder for the domestic animals. Some of these creatures have undergone an island-change through the thousands of years in which they have been isolated from their original mainland stock. As living proof of the effects of ecological isolation we have the Rhum mouse, the St Kilda mouse, the Orkney vole and so on.

The Scilly shrew represents a creature with no counterpart on the mainland. One of two species on the British List, it has white teeth, unlike all mainland shrews which contain a red pigment. The white-toothed shrews, *Crocidurinae*, live only on Scilly and the Channel islands; possibly descendants of a mainland population which was wiped out after the last glaciation or, more probably, the result of introduction by man, since they are common elsewhere in Europe. On Scilly, the animal has foxy ears and long silky bristles on its tail. Its hunting ground is the tide-tossed kelp on the strandline of exposed beaches. Indeed the strandline is a happy hunting ground for other mammals, as well as insects and birds. Apart from treasure-hunting beachcombers, rats and mice tunnel into the weedy piles searching for sand-hoppers and carrion.

In the Scottish islands, and round the coast of Orkney and Shetland, otters are relatively common, leaving their webbed footprints in the sand. While they are retreating and sadly decreasing in England, their numbers are much healthier in the north, where they are more marine in character, fishing for sea fish and crustaceans close inshore. In areas where they are undisturbed they are to be seen during daylight hours, but otters are masters at concealment, and you need to cultivate your local contacts if you are going to see one.

Skomer is famous for its vole, an island race of the familiar bank vole, and it also has a field mouse of distinction. Although neither of these animals is a separate species in the strict scientific sense, since each can breed with its mainland cousins to produce fertile young, they nevertheless have distinctive features resulting from their adaptation to island life. Both are significantly larger than their mainland cousins, and this feature is true of the small mammal populations of many islands. Bigger is better, certainly in the case of a fight, but it's not entirely clear why island mammals should acquire this characteristic. Perhaps the absence of ground predators has something to do with it.

The Skomer vole is a very attractive creature to meet, and it lives in its favoured bracken habitat in great numbers, thicker on the ground than mainland voles. Apart from being bigger, it

The effect of island isolation: the bigger and redder Skomer vole (bottom) is an island race of the mainland bank vole

is redder in colour, but the most noticeable difference, once you have one in your hand, is the easy-going character of the animal. It is very tame, and inclined to sit up in your palm and gaze into your eyes with a benign expression far removed from the fast escape reactions of a mainland vole.

How did the Skomer vole arrive on the island? There are two theories. One is that it was already established there, a very long time ago, before the sea made Skomer an island. Another is that it was introduced accidentally by way of the agricultural to-and-fro, at some time since the original Iron Age occupation. This second version seems the most likely. Work on island sub-species elsewhere has shown that the physical characteristics of an animal race may undergo evolutionary change in a surprisingly short span of time in conditions of isolation. But the exact nature of the survival value of redness, largeness and tameness is not so easily explained.

It is easy to see the attraction of an island to birds, since an island is in many ways the answer to a seabird's prayer. For a good part of the year sea-going birds have no need of land at all, but for the vital purpose of breeding they must come ashore, since they have yet to find a way to incubate eggs on a seaborne nest. The island attractions are obvious enough – plenty of nest sites, little disturbance and no ground predators. As a result Skomer is one of the best bird islands in Britain, with a breeding population of many thousands.

Not all the visitors to Skomer are ocean-going species. The coastal gulls that spend their days scavenging for offal around the Milford Haven fish docks roost there at night and nest there in the summer season. Commuters like these have many influences on the island life. Probably it was a gull that first introduced the myxomatosis virus to the island, by way of a carrier-flea from a mainland rabbit. And often enough a suspicious growth of garden weeds or farm cereals owes its origin to seeds carried in by gulls and deposited in their pellets.

On the gentle slopes of the plateau are colonies of lesser black-backed gulls. Not so long ago their eggs were collected in great numbers to be sent to the grand hotels in London as delicacies, and during the war they represented a welcome resource to egg-starved Pembrokeshire. Gull nests are everywhere, untidily built on the ground amongst the bracken, each at a comfortable distance from its neighbour, but forming part of a highly sociable community. In the central part of the colony the ground is so battered and trampled by the birds' courtship displays and their coming and going, that even the thrusting bracken is beaten back.

Gulls: greater and lesser black-backed,
herring and kittiwake

The relationship between the birds and the vegetation is very close. Quite apart from the effect of trampling, the enrichment of the ground by nitrogen-rich droppings – guano – encourages a healthy growth of red campion, for instance. The attractive pink flowers of this plant are characteristic of the herring gull and lesser black-back breeding areas, places where there is not too much wind-blown salt spray to content with. Fortunately for campion, it is not much liked by rabbits, which only eat it if they must, and, so long as there is no drought, the plant does well, fed by the bird droppings. Guano greatly enriches the soil, adding phosphates, potash and lime, as well as the nitrogen already mentioned. Add to this the odds and ends of food discarded by the gulls, and the inevitable collection of feathers and eggshells, dead chicks and bits of seaweed, and one way or another the gulls bring a varied collection of things to influence and select the island flora. Only when birds nest in close company, as in a gannetry for instance, does the enrichment and trampling become so intense that all vegetation is eliminated.

At one time there were hundreds of great black-backed gulls on the island, but there is no doubt that these large and highly successful predators were having a detrimental effect on the populations of those species which man, in his wisdom, considers more interesting and welcome. And, since the increase in the gull population is itself a result of man's influence (an increase in the availability of food in sewage farms, tips and fish quays) it has seemed a proper function of island management to control their numbers. As a result of much effort on the part of the warden, the population on Skomer is now maintained at about thirty pairs.

The impressive great black-backs tend to nest on prominent rocky outcrops on the higher ground, perhaps overlooking the sort of gentle bracken slope favoured by lesser black-backs. While the sitting bird incubates the giant eggs, the off-duty bird enjoys a panoramic view from a nearby promontory. When the chicks hatch they tend to stay close to home, provided they are not disturbed, until at a couple of months old they are able to fly independently of their parents. By this time the vicinity of the nest is littered with evidence of past meals – rabbit legs and fish bones – along with regurgitated pellets. This is the sort of place where you'll see the sad remains of puffins and Manx shearwaters which have been sacrificed to the gull family. In the recent past, one of the common sights on Skomer was the remains of shearwaters – two wings and a breast-bone picked clean – but one of the happy results of the gull control has been that the shearwater numbers have increased and now fewer corpses litter the island.

If you weren't in on the secret you would have no idea that on Skomer there are a hundred thousand pairs of Manx shearwaters nesting underneath your feet. There is no daytime sign of them, apart from the burrow entrances, which you might reasonably assume belong to rabbits. Silently occupying their underground homes during the day, they wait for the dark of night to venture out into the open. Although it is superbly at home in flight or on the sea, the shearwater is very much at a disadvantage on land. Because its webbed feet are placed well back on its frame, it waddles about in a rather clumsy fashion, half-helping itself with its wings and disappearing into the safety of the nest chamber with an almost audible sigh of relief. Each pair of birds incubates the eggs on a 'week-on, week-off' shift system, and during its time off, the off-duty bird makes a remarkable journey of 600 to 700 miles (965 to 1125km) to the Bay of Biscay for its staple diet of sardines. On its return, in company with thousands of others, it waits out at sea for darkness to fall, before it risks flying in to the dangers of the island terraces.

One of the magical experiences of Skomer is to stay up late on a dark night in June, listening for the first cautious cackling of the underground shearwaters as they wait for the relief party to appear. Round about midnight, the air begins to fill with the sound of demonic squawking, like a thousand cockerels cut off in their prime, and a torch beam cast upwards catches the occasional glimpse of a soot and whitewash body flashing past. Masters of the air, they crash-land and, grounded, become a half-helpless struggling mess of wings, body and legs. Walking along any of the grassy paths at night you must watch your step, for there are bemused shearwaters everywhere. Bemused they may seem, but they are successful enough as a species. The sky is full of them, and on a good evening, the sea holds a giant raft of many thousands more.

When daylight comes, there is no sign of a live shearwater to be seen. Only the burrow entrances gape open as evidence that there is life underground. And, of course, as well as the shearwaters and rabbits, puffins live a subterranean life as well. The thrift-dominated slopes at the cliff-tops are the chosen site for the puffin villages. Here and there, benefitting from the newly dug soil enriched with guano, patches of stinging nettle and ragwort mark the burrow entrance. And, down below, only just out of sight, a baby puffin fattens on a rich diet of sand eels.

Manx shearwaters visit their island nests under cover of darkness, running the gauntlet of gulls which, given the chance, pick them clean, leaving only the tell-tale breastbone and wings

Puffins have serrations in the roof of their mandibles, making it possible for them to carry up to a dozen slippery sand eels

Razorbill coming in to land, its wings and webbed feet acting as air brakes

During the day there is not much activity at the nest area, but towards evening the puffins gather in rafts close inshore, taking off to perform spectacular flights round and round the bay before plummeting in to land near the burrow. Carrying a full beakload of sand eels, they pose and enjoy the evening air a while before disappearing below ground. I always puzzle over the way they manage to catch and carry so many fish, for the gaily-coloured parrot beak may grasp a row of a dozen at a time. It is obvious enough why they need so many. Sand eels may be solid goodness, but they are on the small side, and a baby puffin must be demanding. It seems that the slight serrations on the upper mandible of the beak operate in close conjunction with the mobile tongue. The bird dives underwater and hunts in the sand eel shoal. Picking off its first fish, it grips the head firmly between the back of the tongue and the mandible. From then on, subsequent fish are packed from the back, as the tongue progressively bends up and grips head after head, until the beak has a full load caught in a vice grip. Then it's back to the nest, a row of sad little tails drooping from either side of the beak.

The congregation of brightly coloured puffins decorating the cliff banks is one of the main attractions of Skomer. With their short narrow wings and rapid-beating, fast flight, they whirr about the inshore waters with the carefree air of clockwork toys. While the puffins prefer the gentle cliff slopes, the other two common auks, the razorbills and guillemots, choose the crevices and ledges of the sheer cliff faces, sometimes in enormous numbers. Along with the kittiwake gulls which cluster thickly along the faults, shakes and bedding planes of the vertical cliffs, they form the sea-bird cities that have such an overwhelming impact on the visitor.

Sea-going birds which, again, are at a disadvantage on land, the auks confine their activities ashore to the immediate vicinity of the nest, flying in with webbed feet outstretched as air-brakes in a delicate stalling manoeuvre. Guillemots are the most numerous. Standing upright, penguin fashion, almost shoulder to shoulder on any suitable ledge, they have a slender pointed bill, a smooth chocolate-brown head and upper parts. Incubating a single pear-shaped egg, which is designed not to roll off the ledge if disturbed, they find safety in numbers and a common cause. All members of the colony tend to lay their eggs at the same time, so the birds act almost with a single purpose, sticking close together in order to fight off predators and to benefit from group strength. The chicks huddle together on their precarious ledge, never walking more than a few token

inches. Then the day comes when they all take off and leave the ledge for the first solo flight, gliding down to the safety of the all-embracing sea. The few birds left behind are likely to be snatched up by the constantly watchful gulls, ravens and jackdaws, an example of natural selection in action.

Razorbills, with their deeper, thinner bills, are black where guillemots are brown, and although they nest nearby, they tend to have slightly different site preferences. Where the guillemots nest shoulder to shoulder on the exposed ledges, the razorbills are more inclined to hide themselves under boulders, or to half hide in crevices and corners. They may go for holes in scree-slopes or group themselves amongst boulders. Nonetheless, if the country suits them, they may be present in fair numbers. Like that of the guillemot, the nest consists more of a site than a construction, but there may be a few token pieces of vegetation, or a couple of stones alongside the egg. Being less thick on the ground, razorbills suffer more from the attentions of gulls, but they seem able to fend off the jackdaws.

The seemingly endless toll of auks taken by oil pollution and drowned in fish-nets makes it hard to believe the scientists' contention that auk populations remain at a fairly stable level. There is no doubt that in the twentieth century we are seeing a diminution of their numbers at the southern end of the breeding range, in the bottom half of the UK. One of the distressing results of the auks' predilection for leisurely migration, spending a great deal of time socialising on the water as they travel from the western Mediterranean to the northern breeding places, is that they tend to swim into oil slicks. The result is inevitable, as with clogged feathers and oil-burned lungs they die in large numbers. They also succumb to the increased numbers of gulls, and it may be that they are affected by changes in fish distribution associated with the general temperature rise of our twentieth-century sea. In the south of Britain, many old-established puffin colonies are now gone forever, while the guillemots and razorbills just hold on by their beaks to ancestral breeding sites in the Isles of Scilly and the Westcountry.

Happily, most of the birds you can see on Skomer are doing well, even increasing in numbers. Thirty years or so ago, when I first visited the island, fulmars were just beginning to breed. Now there are over 200 pairs, and the sight of those thick-necked soarers with the straight wings riding the cliff thermals is now a common but still joyful experience. And, though they don't nest on Skomer itself, the gannets, the most spectacular of all north Atlantic seabirds, can be seen every day through the

Three common island-nesting auks: *top to bottom* razorbill, guillemot and puffin

163

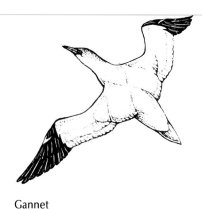

Gannet

breeding season, because on the neighbouring island of Grassholm, only a few miles to the west, there is a thriving gannetry. When I flew over Grassholm in a light aircraft in early June 1978, the whole of the northern half of the island was white with the sitting birds, 20,000 of them. At the breeding place, gannets build their nest mounds at a carefully calculated beak-striking distance from each other. In the face of constant trampling and a powerful rain of guano, no vegetation can survive and the whole area is a sea of white, at least from a distance. Close to, the gold-capped heads, vicious beaks and forward-looking blue eyes set on top of a large white body are a striking sight. Twenty thousand of them makes an overwhelming spectacle – a true sea-bird city. By 1988, there were 27,000 pairs.

Away from the breeding island, gannets make a living as plunge divers, hurtling down from the sky to chase mackerel or pilchards, cushioning the force of the impact with a padded breast. Yet although they are truly at home at sea, gannets, like petrels, kittiwakes and auks, can survive only with the sort of breeding safety afforded by an island, the most rewarding of all natural habitats.

9

The Living Sea

At first sight the sea appears no more than a great expanse of water. Cup your hands for a sample and the result looks as clear as tap water, but there is a different feel to it, and most certainly a different taste. Take a couple of gallons and boil it dry over a beach fire, and you will produce the best part of a cupful of excellent, if rather smoky, sea-salt. The off-white crystalline rime that you scrape from the pan will be mostly sodium chloride, but there will be small quantities of other chemicals and traces of almost any mineral you care to mention.

The nutrient salts, in solution, maintain a huge quantity of plant growth. Whereas on land our familiar plants derive their nutriment from the soil, in the open sea the plants drift in rootless fashion and absorb the phosphates and nitrates that surround them. Tiny and almost invisible to the naked eye, they co-exist in vast quantities with microscopic animals, always near the surface, where they can take advantage of the sunlight to build up sugar supplies, using the carbon dioxide breathed out by the animals which, in turn, live off the plant pasture and benefit from the oxygen it produces.

Together, these plants and animals are known as *plankton*, and their characteristic is that they inhabit the surface regions and drift freely at the mercy of the current. Both plant and animal members of the plankton have some power of movement, though, for without it they would inevitably sink, and in sinking out of reach of sunlight they would die. Some have the capacity to vary the proportions of water and fats in their bodies, using the buoyancy of oil to float themselves up to the surface. Some have long spines or feather-like processes

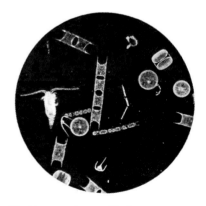

Plankton, much magnified

165

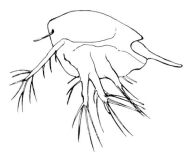

Nauplius larva of the acorn barnacle, *Balanus balanoides* (enlarged); after its drifting period in the plankton, the larva attaches itself to a hard surface, develops protective plates and uses its legs to scoop food particles from the passing current

that reduce the rate at which they sink by increasing frictional resistance. And some of the animals can actively propel themselves upward. Some of the jellyfishes, for example, the largest and most visible of the plankton animals, can jet-propel themselves through the water using muscular force, while others stay at the surface by providing themselves with floats in the shape of bladders, like the Portuguese man-o'-war.

The surface-drifting plant community is known as *phytoplankton* and its animal counterpart *zooplankton*. And these two divisions, each dependent on the other and nourished by gases and salts, are the vital foundation stones for higher life in the sea.

To gain some idea of the teeming life in the surface layer of the sea, I towed a cone-shaped net made of fine nylon for just a few minutes in the waters of Plymouth Sound. Hauled back on board, the interior of the net was coated with a layer of sludge. Carefully scraped off and transferred to a jar of seawater, it was immediately clear that the 'sludge' was full of life. Little creatures jumped and darted about the water. When a drop of it was put under the microscope, the varied shapes were fascinating. Most of the specimens were transparent, but nevertheless full of interest. The plant life was represented by the single-celled diatoms and dinoflagellates, waving their tiny whiplashes in the constant task of maintaining depth. The animals were larval forms of fish, crustaceans and molluscs. Many easily recognisable barnacle larvae were there.

Most of the animals of the sea, whether they are worms, starfishes, crabs, snails, or fishes, start their lives as larvae, drifting with and feeding on the plant pasture. A very large percentage of them end their lives there as well, eaten by something larger; but one of the great advantages of this way of life is that it ensures dispersal at the juvenile stage of creatures which in their adult form will be of a sedentary nature, perhaps even to the extent of being physically attached to a permanent home site.

The fact that a very large percentage of the plankton is eaten by something larger is no accident; it is part of the fundamental economy of the sea. An animal larva may eat some of the phytoplankton, only to be eaten itself by a small fish. The fish then forms part of a mackerel's breakfast, and the mackerel is eaten for dinner by a shark, and thus we have a classic 'food chain'. At the top of each food chain comes the biggest predator, say a killer whale, but in due course he too will die and his decaying remains form food for the plankton, and the cycle is revitalised.

Sometimes the phytoplankton growth may be so prolific that it imparts a definite colour to the sea, perhaps red or yellow. These plankton blooms, for instance 'red tides', may have a disastrous effect because their potentially poisonous mineral contents may be concentrated in the animals that eat too much of them. This in turn may cause subsequent distress, or even death, to animals higher up the food chain. Thus sea-birds, which have eaten molluscs containing high concentrations of toxic dinoflagellates, have been found dead on the shore. People who have eaten cockles or mussels affected by the 'red tide' may suffer serious, or even fatal, attacks of bellyache. The molluscs are apparently unaffected, simply acting as agents for poisons, which they pass on to predators.

The pastures of the sea have their seasons in much the same way as those of the land, although their progression is not seen so clearly by us sea-watchers. The major influences, as on land, are the changes in day-length and temperature associated with the solar cycle. In spring the plants multiply and thrive on the extra light, then in summer, triggered by the warmth, the animals release their spawn to feed on the rich pasture, so that in summer zooplankton is in the ascendant. When the autumn gales stir up the sea-bed and bring a flush of fresh nutrient-rich debris to the surface the phytoplankton enjoys a brief extra period of flowering. Then in winter the period of plenty is over and, as on land, the sea animals face the time of test, only the fittest passing the selection board and surviving to continue their life-cycle. Nevertheless the sea seasons are not so marked as those ashore, and one of the great advantages of a marine existence is that it offers a reasonably stable environment, where temperature change, for instance, is slow. While the hottest days on land may be in June, it is August/September before the sea achieves its greatest warmth. No wild daily fluctuations here.

The plankton plants and animals are at the mercy of tidal currents, but the two other great divisions of life at sea have a certain independence. The *nekton* comprises all those animals that have the facility of swimming, and the *benthos* includes those animals living on the sea bed, taking advantage of the rain of organic debris that drifts down from the surface regions. Both divisions include animals from different classes, but in each case fish are the most highly and successfully adapted to the aquatic life. Snails and crabs may crawl about the bottom, stay put or even float, but fish can do all these things, and also enjoy the freedom of the open waters. They have a well developed sense of sight, some even with colour vision, and they have a keen sense of smell, facilities put to good use in finding food and evading enemies. In addition to these they have a lateral line of sensory cells — easily seen as a coloured line on many of the fish found on the fishmonger's slab. These cells help the fish to detect movements and vibrations in the water.

Fish that live on or near the sea-bed are known as *demersal*, while those inhabiting the open waters are of the sea-going *pelagic* species. In science, fish are divided into three classes: the primitive hagfish and lampreys; the cartilaginous sharks, skates and ray; and the 20,000 species of bony fishes.

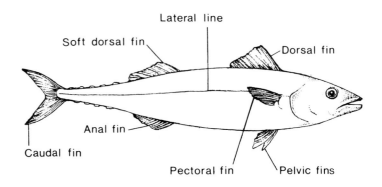

Lateral line

Soft dorsal fin

Dorsal fin

Anal fin

Caudal fin

Pectoral fin

Pelvic fins

Fish topography

The mackerel, with its beautifully streamlined shape, is a typical example of a pelagic bony fish. Its bluntly rounded shape at the head end tapers towards the tail, providing the least resistance to the water and reducing turbulence. This reduced friction is necessary if the fish is to achieve a fair speed through the dense medium of water. Every feature of the fish is designed to produce a surface that offers no irregularities or protruberances to create turbulence. Its mouth closes tight, its eyes and gill covers fit flush, and the body fins operate from slight depressions into which they may fold almost flat when the fish is moving at maximum speed. The body scales are small and smooth, and the whole surface is covered with a mucus slime which helps to grease its passage through the water. The resultant speed allows it not only to chase and capture prey efficiently, but also to escape from trouble.

The fish's fins serve important and distinctive purposes. The dorsal and anal fins are concerned with stabilising the body and countering any tendency to yaw. The paired fins behind and below the head are surfaces controlling pitch and elevation, and of course the tail fin is the propulsion unit, the fishy version of a boat's screw. In order to maintain position at a given depth, many bony fish have trim tanks — controllable buoyancy chambers known as air bladders, or sometimes swim bladders. Mackerel hunt in open water, but a lot of bony fish live on the bottom in shallow water. These demersal fish, of which the plaice is a good example, have evolved a flat shape more suited to their life-style. In order to blend inconspicuously with their background, they lie on their sides. This would render one eye inoperative, but in the course of time the fish's head – eyes and all – has altered its position in such a way that both eyes look upwards from the exposed side. While the fish's underside is more or less white, where it will be out of sight anyway, the upper, exposed surface is camouflaged with colours, spots and blotches to suit the sandy or muddy background. In order to swim, the fish undulates in a waveform, skimming and gliding close to the bottom. Since its prey is usually worms, crustaceans and molluscs, it has no requirement for speed in hunting, and to evade its own enemies it relies on camouflaged stillness. It has also perfected the trick of wiggling its marginal fins at the last moment before it settles, throwing up a flurry of sand which then drops to provide extra cover on its exposed side.

Yet another life-style is demonstrated by the gurnards, fish that rely on neither speed nor camouflage to thwart their attackers, but protect themselves with bony plates and fearsome spines. These remarkable fishes 'walk' over the sea bed in search of food. Two or three of the rays of their pectoral fins are extra long, forming free-ranging feelers that probe and explore amongst the weed and stones, a process which may be seen in action in any aquarium.

The most remarkable of all feeding techniques must surely be that of the angler fish. This, too, has a precociously developed ray, one only, the first ray of the dorsal fin, which has migrated to the front of the fish's head and is canted forward in such a way that it projects ahead of the mouth. Attached to the end of this 'rod' there is a little rag of tissue that acts as bait – so the fish is fully equipped with a fishing rod and a

Unsuspecting tube worm about to be attacked by a hunting plaice

Angler fish

169

lure as well. Lying on the bottom, well camouflaged against the gravel, the angler flicks the lure about to simulate the jerking movement of a small sea creature. When a suitable prey fish comes to investigate, the lure is flicked downwards, towards the angler's mouth. The prey moves in to take the lure, which is then withdrawn to safety as the truly enormous gape of the angler fish opens wide to allow an inrush of water, complete with the unfortunate prey. The angler may grow to more than 3ft (1m) in length, and while it may not appear to us the most beautiful fish in the sea, it nevertheless serves us well under a false name. Many anglers are caught in trawl nets, and the dense white flesh of the tail end is cut into small pieces to arrive on the restaurant table in the guise of 'scampi'.

Like most bony fish, the angler reproduces by spawning, when the female produces a mass of eggs, gathered together in a mucus raft, and fertilised externally by the male's sperm, or milt. The extraordinary number of eggs produced by fishes, often many million from a single female, helps to swell the seasonal ranks of the plankton animals, and, as is the case with all animals which produce large numbers, most of the young are destined for an early death as food for other, larger, fishes.

The male shark's 'claspers', grooved appendages of the pelvic fins which, when inserted into the female's cloaca, provide a route for the seminal fluid

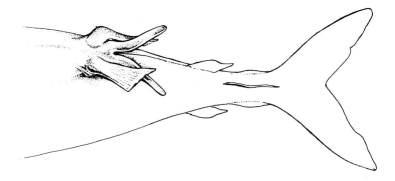

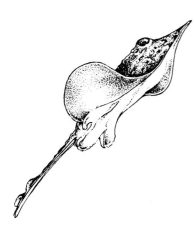

Rays spend most of their time on the sea bed, but are able to 'fly' through the water using their enlarged pectoral fins as wings

This reproductive generosity is not at all characteristic of the other great class of fishes, the Selachians, which includes sharks, dogfish, skates and rays. The female's eggs are fertilised internally by the male in an act of sexual union, and the resulting little fish lives for some time on a diet of yolk in the egg-sac before venturing into the open sea. Another major difference between these fish and the bony fishes is that they have no air bladder. They maintain a slightly negative buoyancy that can be overcome with ease when the powerful tail thrusts the fish forward.

The rays, skates and dogfish spend most of their time on the seabed, hunting crustaceans, molluscs and other fish. The skates and rays are specially flattened for bottom living, with greatly enlarged pectoral fins, which serve to flap the fish through the water in a matter that is closer to flying than swimming. They seem sluggish, but are perfectly able to move quickly when they are after prey, which they smother with their bodies, feeding at leisure by way of a mouth slit placed well back under the head.

Sharks have a fearsome reputation, hardly deserved, as 'wolves of the sea'. But some of them, for instance the blue shark, which is found commonly off the coasts of the south-west, are certainly voracious predators. Built for speed, they have a powerful tail fin, and their streamlining is carried to the extent that the mouth is tucked away underneath so that the blunt snout can present a smooth hydrodynamic entry to the water. The mouth is full of sharp teeth, which are modified versions, enlarged and erect, of the scales that cover the whole body. In effect the shark's outer skin is tucked back to form a mouth, and in the tucked-in area, the scales present themselves as teeth. The teeth project back slightly into the mouth to make it even more difficult for the prey to get out.

However, for all its reputation, you are unlikely to have your

Common British sharks: *top to bottom* blue, porbeagle, mako and basking

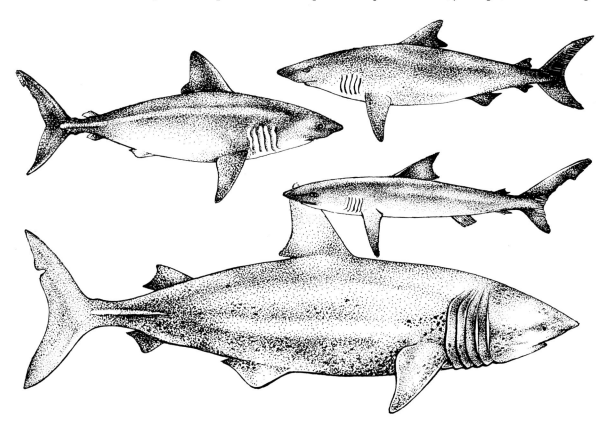

171

leg chopped off at one stroke by a blue shark, and the self-satisfaction of the shark-anglers at having conquered this terror of the sea is somewhat exaggerated. You are even less likely to lose a leg to the magnificent basking shark, because it feeds entirely on plankton. It cruises at the surface, its open mouth sampling thousands of tons of seawater every hour, sieving the plankton out with the fine-tooth comb of its gill rakers. A placid and inoffensive creature (so long as you are not a member of the plankton community) it is a common sight off western coasts in the summer. Skin-divers can swim close to the great fish (which may, exceptionally, be as much as 40ft (12m) long) without difficulty, if they behave with caution. The only time a basker may become dangerous is when it 'sounds' in a panic; then its sheer bulk and lashing tail may capsize the small boat that may have surprised it. Like the other selachians, this fish has no swim bladder but it maintains its surface station by manipulating the buoyancy of its massive, oily liver.

Often you will see a party of herring gulls on the water where a basking shark is performing its lazy circles. Presumably they derive some benefit from its activity, though they never seem to be actively feeding at the time. On other occasions, when for example a mackerel shoal is chasing hordes of tiny fish at the surface, the gulls will join in the hunt. Gulls are opportunist feeders, having a go at anything, and they are the common companies of any trip round the bay. In summer terns may be fishing the surface waters, too. Common and Arctic terns, with their swallow-tails, or sandwich terns, with their heavier bodies and yellow-tipped bills, all patrol the inshore waters, ready to pounce on a surface titbit.

The most spectacular 'pouncer' is the gannet, which plunge-dives on its prey – a mackerel perhaps – from a great height. First marking its chosen prey from the air, it closes its wings to accelerate headlong. Specially adapted for this activity, with forward vision, gannets strike the surface with great force, sending up a tremendous splash and continuing the dive in an underwater chase using feet and wings. The catch may be swallowed underwater or it may be brought to the surface. Usually the dive is brief and the bird rises, takes off, then circles to dive again. Though you may see them close inshore, especially in stormy weather, gannets usually hunt far out to sea. Whiter-than-white, their long wings tipped with black, they are as big as a turkey and easily recognised.

Sea ducks enjoy the feeding in sheltered coastal waters outside the breeding season, and they are common enough. Shy birds, seldom ashore, they group together on the water in rafts which may consist of hundreds of birds. They are divers, swimming to the sea-bed for molluscs and crustaceans in dives that usually last about half a minute. Common scoters are likely sightings. The drakes have a striking glossy black plumage, with a prominent yellow patch on a black bill, but you will be lucky to see that; usually they take off and fly away in a party long before you get close to them. On the water they have a buoyant posture, but when alarmed they are able to sink down and make themselves inconspicuous.

Other diving birds, like shags and cormorants, tend to maintain this sunken posture, swimming with what any sailor would regard as a dangerously low freeboard – not much ship above the surface! But there is a real advantage here for the birds. As divers, they are more efficient when they carry less surface air down with them, so they have plumage which is intentionally less waterproof than that of most birds. Whereas ducks, for instance, retain a layer of warmed air between their skin and their plumage, shags and cormorants use the wet-suit principle employed by human divers. The disadvantage is that they do get wet, and therefore need to dry their plumage after diving, in order to regain full flight capability and to restore the thermal qualities of their feathers.

In spring, both shags and cormorants are common coastal breeding species, although their requirements differ significantly. The cormorants choose to nest sociably in colonies on rocky slopes, whereas the shags nest in solitary isolation in some dark crevice or cranny. Both feed on the plentiful shoal-water fish like pollack and wrasse, but outside the breeding season cormorants tend to forsake the coast for the more sheltered waters of the estuaries.

Seals prey on fish, too. They tend to find themselves a convenient resting place, a sand-bank in the case of common seals or a smooth and easily reached rocky ledge in the case of the grey seals, and go fishing when the rising tide forces them out of bed. I once watched a cow grey seal surface in shallow water, with a large flatfish gripped in her teeth. Lying comfortably in an upright position in the water, she proceeded to eat it at leisure, holding the carcass between her two mobile front flippers just as if she were sitting at table.

As divers, seals are well adapted. They can stay under water for several minutes of active chasing, using the full power of their hind flippers, but if they choose simply to sleep on the sea bed they have the facility to reduce their heart rate – and therefore their rate of oxygen use – in order to rest undisturbed for twenty minutes or so. When the level of oxygen in the blood drops too low, they rise gently to the surface to flush out the system and take in a fresh charge of air. Then they sink slowly to the bottom again – all this without waking up! As a warm-blooded mammal, the seal's provision for heat insulation includes a thick pelt of fur outside and a solid layer of blubber inside the skin.

No one is likely to mistake a seal for a fish, yet whales of all sorts are frequently misidentified in this way. Unlike the seals, which spend a great deal of time ashore (and indeed must come ashore to drop their pups), the whales are mammals that spend their whole life immersed in the sea. They have forsaken any kind of fur coat (which has the disadvantage that it eventually becomes waterlogged) because they would have no way of drying it regularly as the seal does. Instead they rely on the insulating properties of blubber to maintain their body temperature. In shape they are very fish-like, for the excellent reason that the fish shape is the most efficient form for travelling in water. Like fish and seals, they drive themselves by means of tail fins, but in the case of the whales these are attached horizontally, so that the forward motion through the water is achieved by an up and down stroke instead of the fish-like side to side movement. Whales (known in biological

Whales of British waters: *top to bottom* killer, pilot, dolphin and porpoise

parlance as Cetaceans) come in two kinds, those that have teeth and are active predators on fish, birds, seals and other whales; and whalebone whales which trawl the sea with open mouths, sieving shrimps from enormous quantities of water. Off the coast of Britain we are most likely to see the smaller whales, the dolphins and porpoises, although killer whales and pilot whales are not infrequent visitors. Fishermen in west Cornwall like to tell of the days on which a killer whale, longer than the 20ft (6m) crabber the men are working in, comes alongside and raises a beady eye to see what is going on. Though the danger from killers is much exaggerated, it is only prudent to give them a wide berth.

Whales have small eyes, since their principal fish-catching sense is not vision but a form of echo-location, in which they listen for the returning echo of sound signals that they themselves originate. If you ever find yourself diving in the midst of a school of cetaceans, as I have, you will hear a continuous rain of high-frequency whistles and clicks, increasing in intensity as they approach through the murky water – an unnerving experience when the sound is made by a carnivorous mammal larger than yourself.

Echo-location, using a visual display, is one of the prime techniques used nowadays by another fish-hunting mammal, man. Ever since the year dot, man has been a keen fisherman, and has played a full part in harvesting the bounty of the sea. Harvesting is, perhaps, a wrong word to use, since sea fishing is more a matter of hunting, there being no question of sowing that we may reap. We have come a long way since the days when Mesolithic man fashioned harpoons and bone hooks and hammered shellfish off rocks with stones. But, apart from salmon and certain shellfish, notably the oyster, we have not yet cracked the problem of farming the fertile acres of the sea commercially. Though the fishing industry today is highly sophisticated, it is still based on the crudest principles of scoop, scrape, entangle and snare. The vessels used for the job have changed little, though their propulsion units and gear have changed a lot. The most significant change came at the turn of the century, when steam tugs were first used to tow a fleet of sailing trawlers to the fishing grounds (thus increasing their working time) and then to bring them home again to market. By the end of World War I most large fishing boats operated under steam of their own, while the inshore day boats were still dependent on sail. Nowadays, when oil engines reign supreme, the only sails to be seen are the occasional steadying mizzen, apart from delightful anachronisms like the Helford River

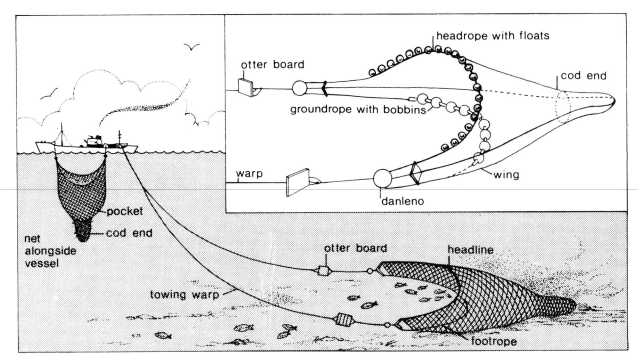

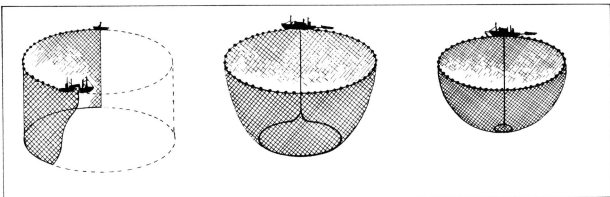

Top Trawlers tow an open-mouthed net along the sea-bed to disturb and engulf demersal fish; *middle* purse-seiners 'bag' a sample of surface water for pelagic fish; *right* long-liners catch bottom fish like ling with baited hook and line

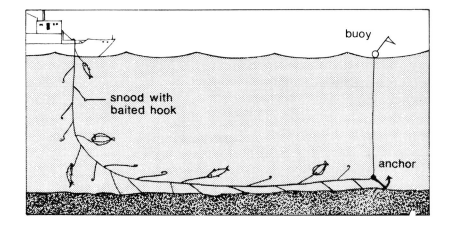

oyster fleet, which must, by law, fish under sail alone, this providing a taste of bygone beauty.

Fishing boats come in all shapes and sizes, tested in severe conditions and adapted to their different jobs in much the same way as their prey have evolved for their way of life. Open boats, up to about 42ft (13m) in length, crabbers and long-liners, often working from open beaches or natural harbours, operate close inshore on a daily basis for shellfish, or for ling and conger, ray and turbot. Much larger, and vastly more expensive, purse-seiners work away for days at a time, surrounding whole shoals with their nets, then storing the catch in chilled seawater tanks. However, the most developed of the fishing vessels is the trawler. In biological terms, it is a voracious predator – highly seaworthy, very powerful and with a high load capacity. A typical Newlyn vessel, the *Rose of Sharon*, is built for dual purpose working, side or stern trawling. Some 65ft (20m) in overall length, she works the Western Approaches from Start Point to Scilly, fishing mackerel in winter and 'flats' in the summer. Just forward of her wheelhouse is a powerful winch with a thirteen-ton pull, the sort of power needed to deal with heavy trawl warps towing a net that may be as big as a rugby pitch along the seabed for three or four hours at a time. The mouth of the trawl is kept open by a row of floats along its top edge and by the otter boards, whose movement through the water splays the net out sideways. At the base of the net, a heavy foot chain stirs up the sea bed, disturbing demersal fish, which fall into the mouth of the net and are swept down to the cod end. The trawl net is towed by heavy lines – warps – which are led from the winch by way of heavy metal supports – gallows – at the side or the stern of the vessel (hence 'side' or 'stern' trawlers).

When the trawling period is over, the vessel heaves to and the big winch turns, hauling in the warps. When the otter boards surface they are secured to the gallows, then the mouth end of the net is piled on the deck. When the cod end breaks the surface, bloated with an assortment of fish, kittiwakes and fulmars swarm in to enjoy their share of the catch. Large quantities of undersized fish and unwanted species are destined to be swept overboard when the catch is sorted. For the naturalist, the major interest of a trip with a trawling crew is the excitement of sorting through this 'trash'.

If the trawling has been close inshore there will be oarweed fronds, swarming with life, worms, molluscs and seamats, and there will be sea urchins and starfish and brittlestars a-plenty. The deeper you go, the more surprises there are in the catch –

enough to keep you occupied for hours. Never pass up the chance to join a trawlerman for a day, for there is almost nothing to beat the excitement of the random collection of sea life pouring over the ship's deck when the crewman releases the cod-end knot!

Beam trawlers tow by way of massive outboard booms that are stayed to the mainmast and pull two trawls, one each side. They may work for demersal fish or, more likely, for scallops, in which case they use a trawl made of steel mesh, with the foot chain replaced by a fixed metal bar wth teeth, which digs up the top layer of sand, scallops and all.

In terms of efficiency, trawlers work best when they act as a fleet, locating and maintaining contact with the fish shoals, so that while the day-boat men may still work from coves and harbours, sometimes little more than natural shelters, the heavier end of the industry has concentrated on the relatively few places which have developed the necessary specialised facilities to serve large fleets. A man-made breakwater and long quays complete with ice factory, fish market and rail terminal are the order of the day. Most capital investment is concentrated on the 'distant water' ports like Hull and Grimsby. At Hull, where until recently half the fish caught by British trawlers was landed, there is a quay a mile in length, yet in the past it has been not an inch too long. But fortunes in the fishing industry, like the fish stocks themselves, are liable to violent change, and because of overfishing in the Arctic, there are big trawlers lying idle in many east coast ports.

The pattern of fishing varies greatly with the coastal geography. In the north-east, the fish market demonstrates endless rows of cod and haddock. At Lowestoft, the fish boxes are filled with plaice. By contrast, at Brixham or Plymouth or Newlyn in the south-west, the landings on a single day may encompass an astonishing variety of species. On a successful July day in Newlyn the auctioneers may sell over thirty species including, as a random sample, ling, bass, conger, spurdog, dogfish, tope, pouting, cuckoo and thornback ray, turbot, brill, angler fish, pollack, bream, red and tub gurnard, angel fish, saithe, cod, plaice, lemon and dover sole, megrim, hake, haddock, John Dory, porbeagle and blue shark, also molluscs such as squid and octopus. And not to mention the crabs, crawfish, lobsters and scallops that are landed in the same port but marketed elsewhere. Of some 160 sea fishes regarded by the Ministry of Agriculture Fisheries and Food as common in British waters, only thirty-four are listed as commercially edible, while many others remain to have their day when

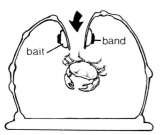

Traditional 'inkwell' crab pot; the bait is usually skewered inside the neck of the pot, and the crab smells its way in

prejudices can be overcome. Overcome they will be, as in the past, when dogfish, previously regarded as a pest, found itself on the slab as 'flake' and the tabby-striped catfish (regarded as so ugly that it was skinned at the dockside, before sale) was presented as 'rock-salmon', 'rock turbot' or 'woof'.

The fish trade, not unreasonably, classifies all fish as either 'round' or 'flat', but it is one of the pleasures of a visit to the fish market to try and unravel the wild intricacies of fish-slab nomenclature. Several species, including catfish and spurdogs, may reach your table as 'rock salmon', and several species lend their flesh to the simulation of 'scampi', a name which belongs by rights to the Norway prawn, *Nephrops*. The lesser spotted dogfish *Scyliorhinus caniculus* may also commonly be known as nursehound, but in Newlyn it is firmly called a mergie, while the Fisheries officers stick out for huss. A saithe is a coalfish is a coley. The textbook angel fish is the fishmonger's monk fish unless you are in Newlyn where it is a fiddler fish. And others say a monk fish is an angler fish anyway. It is a delightful maze!

As rock salmon, the spurdog *Squalus acanthias* is in great demand by the fish and chip trade, now that the traditional round fish species are no longer so plentiful. Grimsby, the centre of the UK dogfish trade, landed 1,719 tonnes in 1975, but unfortunately the increased fishing is having a bad effect on stocks, with increased numbers of small fish being taken. Inevitably this heavy fishing of immature stock will accelerate the decline which has been evident since records were begun in 1960. Overfishing has already seen the decline of the herring, whose spawning stock is at a low ebb. And while the sprat has to a certain extent filled the gap, at least in the north-east, one wonders how long sprat stocks can withstand the onslaught.

In the south-west the mackerel is now under siege, and indeed with the herring it is a good example of the fluctuating fortunes of the fishing industry. In the early fifties herrings accounted for 87% of the total pelagic catch. By 1975, in a total catch which remained constant, only 11% were herrings, while sprats, with mackerel coming up close behind, shared 86%. By 1976 herrings were down to 9% of the total, while mackerel at 44% had overtaken the 41% of sprats. Mackerel were heading for a boom or bust, along with the freezer-trawlers which, denied the Icelandic waters, converged on the fish-rich south-west. Well over 95% of the English mackerel catch is taken in the coastal waters of Cornwall and south Devon, mostly in the period October to March. In 1975, for instance, the total Westcountry catch by both British and foreign vessels was 492,000 tonnes. Whether the stocks can

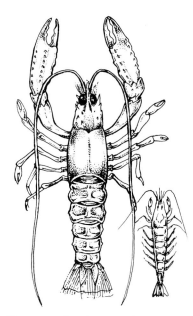

Size comparison between the scampi prawn *Nephrops* (left) and the common shrimp (right)

withstand increased fishing remains to be seen, but there has been a dramatic increase in the catch since that time, with a continuing influx of pelagic trawlers from ports outside Devon and Cornwall. Certainly the success of the inshore handline fishermen has been overshadowed by what must seem a tidal wave of competition.

Fisheries scientists work hard to learn something of the economy of the sea, with a view to knowing how best we may harvest the potentially inexhaustible supplies of protein. But all too often their efforts are hampered by the greed of man the fisherman, whose concern is often to take everything he can get, without thought of the future.

Appendices

TOOLS OF THE TRADE

One of the pleasures of coastal outings is the freedom from restraint. No one expects you to wear a tie or neatly pressed trousers when you are tramping the beaches. Yet the animals that live on the coast are specially equipped for living on the seashore and it makes sense for us, too, to bear some of the problems in mind, and to consider our own equipment very carefully.

If your object is simply to enjoy an easy day, then you will only want to carry an anorak of some kind in case the weather turns against you, but if you are likely to be collecting specimens then it makes sense to carry a shoulder bag or small rucksack. Some people take a net with them and perhaps a transparent plastic sandwich box too. This acts as a portable aquarium, enabling you to observe animals in their natural watery environment. When all is said and done, however, there is no doubt that the less gear you carry, the more enjoyable is the day. It is very easy to add a camera and books to the load, which may seem light as you set off, but will become a wearisome burden before the sun sets.

It can on occasion be very difficult to decide what to wear on your feet. Although there is great pleasure in walking the sandflats, and even rocky ledges, in bare feet, there are dangers. Quite apart from broken glass and tin cans, there is the possibility of treading on the poisonous spines of a weever fish, although this is only a real danger when paddling at low water spring tides. I prefer well worn plimsolls of a vintage that has worn convenient drain-holes in them. These holes not only let the sea water run out, but also ventilate the toes in a most satisfactory manner. Gumboots are useful in winter, because they allow you to wear a pair of warm socks and – provided you are careful the sea does not slop over the top of them – to keep dry feet, but they have disadvantages. If you are going to do a lot of walking in them they tend to be tiring, but more serious is their lack of grip on the slippery seaweed surfaces of rocky ledges. If you must wear gumboots, then choose the sort made specially for yachtsmen, with flexible soles designed for gripping a heaving deck. However, be warned that in the rough conditions of the shore they have a short, and expensive, life.

Stout boots as used by walkers and climbers have no place in the seashore explorer's kit. Quite apart from the lengthy and tiresome performance of getting them on and off whenever you want to paddle in even a few inches of water, they rapidly fill with sand, which soon grates and produces blisters. The tattiest and simplest canvas-type shoes are probably the best.

Perhaps surprisingly, Ordnance Survey maps rarely find a place in my shore-going day bag. Almost always the actual distance covered is going to be small, so it makes more sense to have a good look at the 1:25,000 map before you set out, so that you do not have to risk getting it baptised with sea water. One of the ever-present problems is that sand and sea water have an uncanny knack of finding their way into everything you carry, and this makes life particularly difficult if you want to carry cameras. It is really vital to protect your photographic gear from drops of salt water, let alone a soaking, because sea water has quite severe corrosive properties. My answer to the problem is to carry optical gear in strong plastic bags, often double-wrapped inside the sort of stout plastic carrier bags that you get from supermarkets and the like. If you are carrying a rucksack of some kind, it makes good sense to throw in a few plastic bags. They weigh practically nothing and are most useful for any number of things, from keeping specimens tidy to keeping your wet bathing trunks away from your sandwiches.

Unless you are a birdwatcher, it may be as well to leave your binoculars at home. Carried round your neck they detract from the sense of freedom on the beach, and carried in your bag they are never ready when you need them most. On the other hand, if you do not have your binoculars with you, then that is bound to be the day when a school of whales blows by, or when the water's edge is alive with waders. For birdwatchers, binoculars are practically a necessity. Most birds protect themselves from their enemies by evasion and will not let you come near, no matter how patient you are. The binoculars, although they present you with a narrower field of view, bring the birds closer in a way that the birds themselves would never permit.

Many people find difficulty in choosing a pair of binoculars, so it may be useful to outline some of the considerations. All binoculars are described in terms of their magnification and the size of the objective lens. Thus 8 × 30 glasses magnify the image eight times (that is an object 800 feet/metres away will appear to be 100 feet/metres away) and have an aperture diameter of 30mm. This last measurement gives an indication of the brightness of the perceived picture, so that an aperture diameter of 25mm will give an appreciably duller picture than one of 40mm. At this point it may seem that, considerations of money apart, the glasses that give the highest possible magnification, coupled with the largest possible aperture diameter, are inevitably the best buy. This is not the case, but unfortunately it is a common misconception which is taken advantage of by mail-order advertisers, who put great stress on high magnification when offering binoculars of doubtful, and in some cases almost non-existent, value.

There are severe problems with high magnification glasses. In order to use them satisfactorily they need to be securely attached to an anchorage such as a tripod. They may be heavy, in which case the tripod needs to be heavy in turn. Any glasses with a magnification greater than 12 × will almost certainly need to be fixed to something, otherwise the image will shake so much that the benefit of the enlargement is lost. If you have a steady hold, you may be able to manage 12 × glasses, but only for a short time. And on a beach there is very rarely a convenient gate or post on which to rest them. Other considerations involve the weight of the binoculars (and bear in mind that by some strange magic they get heavier as the day goes by) and the resolution of the lenses. Resolution is the technical term for the quality and excellence of the optical system, and by and large you get what you pay for.

So beware of high magnification, especially if it is coupled with an inadequate aperture diameter of the objective lens; 15 × 30 glasses might possibly be of some value to a desert nomad, looking at distant objects in bright light, with his recumbent camel to rest on, but they will not be much use watching waders in Britain in December.

To sum up, stick to a magnification of 8 × or 9 × (10 × if you have steady hands) with an aperture diameter of at least 30, preferably 40 and certainly 50 if you choose the 10 ×. Avoid mail-order except in the case of firms advertising in journals like *British Birds* or the RSPB magazine *Birds.* Try out several pairs of binoculars before you choose. For the best possible advice, see J. Flegg's pamphlet *Binoculars, telescopes and cameras for the birdwatcher*, obtainable from the British Trust for Ornithology, Beech Grove, Tring, Herts.

Although there is a bewildering choice of binoculars from which to choose, when you are considering which books to put in your bag there is less difficulty. Since there is no way in which you can carry a complete seashore library with you, you are almost certainly going to confine your choice to a bird and/ or seashore field guide. I always carry the most recent edition of *The Hamlyn Field Guide to the Birds of Britain and Europe*. For shore plants and animals I tend to dither between a longtime favourite, *The Collins Pocket Guide to the Sea Shore*, by John Barret and C, M. Yonge, which is available in a suitably seawaterproof binding, and *The Hamlyn Guide to the Seashore and Shallow Seas of Britain and Europe* by A. C. Campbell, which has the decided merit of a more logical layout, where the pictures are arranged on opposite pages to the relevant text. Both are admirable and practically essential tools for the coast-goer.

There are many other books which could have a treasured place in your library. Perhaps the most useful thing is to suggest some guidelines, but in my experience librarians in any branch of the Public Library system are willing to give advice.

*ANGEL, H. *The World of An Estuary* Faber, 1974

*BARRETT, J. *Life on the Sea Shore* Collins, 1974

CAMPBELL, B. *Birds of Coast and Sea: Britain and Northern Europe* OUP, 1977

CHAPMAN, V. J. *Coastal Vegetation* Pergamon Press, n.e. cased and paperback 1976

CHAPMAN, V. J. *Seaweeds and Their Uses* Methuen, n.e. 1970

*CRAMP, S. *The Seabirds of Britain and Ireland* Collins, 1977

ELTRINGHAM, S. K. *Life in Mud and Sand* ULP, 1971

FISHER, J. and LOCKLEY, R. M. *Seabirds* Collins, 1954 o.p.

FRASER, F. C. *British Whales, Dolphins, and Porpoises* British Museum (Natural History) n.e. 1976

FRIEDRICH, H. *Marine Biology* Sidgwick and Jackson, 1970

GIBSON-HILL, C. A. *A Guide to the Birds of the Coast* Constable, 1976

GREEN, J. *The Biology of Estuarine Animals* Sidgwick and Jackson, 1968 o.p.

*HARDY, SIR A. *The Open Sea* Collins, 2 Vols n.e. 1970–71

HAYMAN, P. et al *Shorebirds* Croom Helm, 1986

LEWIS, J. R. *The Ecology of Rocky Shores* EUP, 1964; Hodder n.e. paperback 1976

*NICHOLS, D. *The Oxford Book of Invertebrates* OUP, 1971

PRATER, A. J. *Estuary Birds* T. and A. D. Poyser, 1981

*RUSSELL, F. S. and YONGE, C. M. *The Seas* Warne, n.e. 1975

STEERS, J. A. *The Sea Coast* Collins, 1954

YONGE, C. M. and THOMPSON, T. E. *Living Marine Molluscs* Collins, 1976

*YONGE, C. M. *The Sea Shore* Collins, n.e. 1966

Strongly recommended

THE COASTAL CODE

In drawing up this code, the Nature Conservancy Council had particularly in mind the activities of educational field courses, skin divers, sea anglers and bait diggers, but the suggestions are equally relevant for all who visit the seashore.

Our coasts are increasingly being used for education, and more and more pressure is being exerted on their plant and animal life. Unless we are careful we will destroy the very features we have come to study and enjoy. If future generations are to enjoy the richness of our shores and shallow seas, remember . . .

DON'T DISTURB
DON'T DESTROY
ACT RESPONSIBLY
FOLLOW THE COUNTRY CODE

Disturbance

Disturbance for many animals can affect their breeding cycles and feeding behaviour and in some instances even cause death.
Do not turn rocks over unnecessarily and always return them to their original position, taking care not to crush animals and plants beneath them.
When taking photographs avoid disturbing the subject and its surroundings and always leave everything as you found it. An animal exposed for a photograph is also exposed to predators.
Trampling can damage sand dunes, cliff tops and salt marshes by destroying their protective covering of plant life.
Spread the area from which you collect bait and always back fill holes you've dug.

Destruction

Demonstrate living material without removing it.
Do not mark animals without expert advice. Bad marking can kill or expose an animal to predators.
Don't collect living plants and animals. Empty shells make the best souvenirs. Identify plants and animals by taking the book to the shore, not the shore to the book.
Sea urchins and sea fans take years to grow. Please leave them alone.
Spear fishing makes fish shy of divers. Don't spearfish for wrasse and other inshore species. Once an area is depleted of fish it may take a long time for them to recolonise it.

Carelessness

Boat fuel will kill marine life, use it with care.
Litter is both dangerous and unsightly; take it home with you.
Spear fishing is dangerous near other water users.
Discarded fishing line and nets can trap and kill sea birds.
If on an educational trip make your visit instructive not destructive, follow the Outdoor Studies Code and the code for Geological Fieldwork.

When recording at sites of special scientific interest or nature reserves, send a copy of your results to the Institute of Terrestrial Ecology, Biological Records Centre, Abbots Ripton, Huntingdon. Also to the appropriate Regional Officer of the Nature Conservancy Council.

The Outdoor Studies Code is obtainable from the Resources Committee of the Council for Environmental Education, 9 Devereux Court, Strand WC2 3JR, and the Code for Geological Field Work from The Geologists' Association, c/o Department of Geology, University College London, Gower Street, London WC1E 6BT.

WRECK LAW

The King shall have wreck of the sea throughout the realm.
17 Edward II c II, S I

In other words, finders are not keepers. Not legally, anyway. In fact it is not even very clear whether or not a wrecker has the right to be on the beach at all. The law relating to **flotsam** (wreck found floating at sea), **jetsam** (wreck that has been cast overboard to lighten the ship in peril) and **lagan** (wreck found cast ashore) is full of pitfalls and anomalies, but the basic premise is that all things found at sea or on the beach belong to somebody. Most of the foreshore is owned by the Crown, but not all of it. Lords of the manor have different rights in different parts of the country, and the records are full of erudite dispute.

The expression 'wreck' has been defined as property cast ashore after shipwreck or found in or on the shores of any tidal water. In addition the definition covers all 'derelict' articles, derelict being a term used to describe property, whether vessel or cargo, which has been abandoned without hope of recovery. From this it follows that most articles found on the shore or retrieved from the sea bed may fall within the definition of wreck.

Wreck is classified as either owned or unclaimed. In both cases the salvor has a duty to inform the Receiver of Wreck. With owned wreck he may claim salvage rights from the owner. In any dispute the Receiver acts as arbiter. Interference with wreck without permission of the owner involves liability to a penalty not exceeding £100. Removing parts of the wreck and not returning them to the owner incurs a penalty of double the value of the wreck.

In the case of unclaimed wreck, the Receiver enters the case in a register and this is known as 'opening a droit'. Unclaimed after one year, the property reverts to the Crown and is sold. In this case the salvor usually gets one third of the proceeds, although there is no legal basis for this figure, which may vary according to the danger of the salvage operation, the degree of skill involved, etc.

Articles that do not come within the definition of wreck come in the same category as lost property. Deck cargo, when washed overboard, becomes lost property, even though the cargo may finish up on the shore. (There is an anomaly in the case of fishing gear. If it is lost overboard it *does* constitute wreck, although no shipwreck need be involved.)

Navigation marks, buoys, etc, when adrift, are not wreck, but lost property, and this same protection applies to anything found within the confines of a harbour or above MHWS level. The theft of lost property is dealt with as an act of common larceny.

So it is clear that, legally, all wreck must be reported. If the property has a likely value of £20 or more the receiver (normally the local Customs Officer) must notify Lloyds. If the wreck is below a certain value, or perishable, and is unclaimed, the officer may sell it, an appropriate award being made to the salvor. The Receiver of Wreck has wide powers. He may requisition vessels or vehicles. He has legal powers to enter private land if he suspects that an offence has been committed. It is his duty to suppress attempts at plunder. And, incidentally, it is an offence even to board a wrecked vessel without the consent of either the Receiver or the owner.

Certain wrecks are of archeological interest, and if you discover anything that might come in this category it should be left undisturbed and reported to the Council for Nautical Archaeology (contacted through the National Maritime Museum at Greenwich), although the Receiver of Wreck must be informed first.

SCIENTIFIC NAMES OF SPECIES MENTIONED IN THIS BOOK

Angler fish *Lophius piscatorius*
Aster, sea *Aster tripolium*
Avocet *Avocetta recurvirostra*

Barnacle, acorn *Balanus sp.*
Barnacle, goose *Lepas anatifera*
Bass *Dicentrarchus labrax*
Bittern *Botaurus stellaris*
Bluebell *Endymion non-scriptus*
Bracken *Pteridium aquilinum*
Brittlestar *Ophrothrix fragilis*
Bunting, cirl *Emberiza cirlus*
Butterfish *Pholis gunnellus*

Cabbage, wild *Brassica oleracea*
Campion, red *Silene dioica*
Campion, sea *Silene maritima*
Celandine, lesser *Ranunculus
    ficaria*
Chiton *Lepidochitona cinereus*
Chough *Pyrrhocorax pyrrhocorax*
Cockle, common *Cardium edule*
Cod *Gadus morhua*
Cord grass *Spartina townsendii*
Cormorant *Phalacrocorax carbo*
Crab, edible *Cancer pagurus*
    hermit *Eupagurus sp.*
    long-clawed porcelain
        Porcellana longicornis
    masked *Corystes cassivelaunus*
    shore *Carcinus maenas*
    spiny spider *Maia squinado*
Crawfish *Palinurus vulgaris*
Crow *Corvus corax*
Curlew *Numenius arguata*

Dogfish, greater spotted
        Scyliorhinus stellaris
    lesser spotted
        Scyliorhinus caniculus
Dolphin, bottle-nosed
        Tursiops truncatus
Dove, rock *Columba livia*
Dunlin *Calidris alpina*

Eel, common *Anguilla anguilla*
    conger *Conger conger*

Fennel *Foeniculum vulgare*
Fescue, red *Festuca sp.*
Flounder *Platichthys flesus*
Fox *Vulpes vulpes*
Fulmar *Fulmarus glacialis*
Furrow, peppery *Scrobicularia
    plana*

Gannet *Sula bassana*
Gaper, sand *Mya arenaria*
Glasswort *Salicornia europaea*
Godwit, black-tailed *Limosa
    limosa*
    bar-tailed *Limosa lapponica*
Goose, barnacle *Branta leucopsis*
    brent *Branta bernicla*
Grass, lyme *Elymus arenarius*
    marram *Ammophila arenaria*
    sand couch *Agropyron
    junceiforme*
Gribble *Limnoria lignorum*
Guillemot *Uria aalge*
Gull, black-headed *Larus
    ridibundus*
    greater black-backed *Larus
    marinus*
    herring *Larus agentatus*
    kittiwake *Rissa tridactyla*
    lesser black-backed *Larus fuscus*
Gurnard, red *Trigla cuculus*

Haddock *Melanogrammus
    aeglefinus*
Harrier, marsh *Circus aeruginosus*
Hawkbit, hairy *Leontoplon
    hispiclus*
Heron, grey *Ardea cinerea*
Herring *Clupea harengus*

Ice-plant *Carpobrotus edulis*
Ivy, ground *Glechoma hederacea*

Jackdaw *Corvus monedula*
Jack sail-by-the-wind *Velella
    velella*
John Dory *Zeus faber*

Knot *Calidris canatus*

Lark, sky *Alauda arvensis*
Lavender, sea *Limonium vulgare*
Limpet, common *Patella vulgata*
Ling *Molva molva*
Lobster *Homarus vulgaris*
Lugworm *Arenicola marina*

Mackerel *Scomber scombrus*
Mallard *Anas platyrhynchos*
Mallow, tree *Lavatera arborea*
Moth, wainscot *Leucania litoralis*
Mouse, Rhum *Apodemus sp.*
Mouse, St Kilda *Apodemus sp.*
Mullet *Crenimugil labrosus*

Newt, smooth *Triturus vulgaris*

Oarweed *Laminaria digitata*
Octopus *Octopus vulgaris*
Osprey *Pandion haliaetus*
Otter *Lutra lutra*
Owl, short-eared *Asio flammeus*
Oystercatcher *Haematopus
    astralegus*

Peregrine *Falco peregrinus*
Periwinkle, common *Littorina
    littorea*
    flat *Littorina littoralis*
    rough *Littorina saxatilis*
    small *Littorina neritoides*
Piddock, common *Pholas dactylus*
Pigeon *Columba palumba*
Pine, Monterey *Pinus radiata*
Pipit, rock *Anthus spinoletta*
Plaice *Pleuronectes platessa*
Plantain, buck's-horn *Plantago
    coronopus*
Plover, ringed *Charadrius
    hiaticula*
Pollack *Pollachius pollachius*
Porpoise, common *Phocaena
    phocaena*
Portuguese man-o-war
        Physalia physalia
Puffin *Fratercula arctica*
Purslane, sea *Halimione
    portulacoides*

Rabbit *Oryctolagus cuniculus*
Ragworm *Nereis virens*
Ragwort *Senecio jacobaea*
Raven *Corvus corax*
Ray, electric *Torpedo marmorata*
  sting *Dasyatis pastinaca*
  thornback *Raja clavata*
Razorbill *Alca torda*
Razorshell *Ensis sp.*
Redshank *Tringa totanus*
Redstart, black *Phoenicurus ochruros*
Reedling, bearded *Panurus biarnicus*

Salmon, Atlantic *Salmo salar*
Samphire, rock *Crithmum maritimum*
Sanderling *Calidris alba*
Sand gaper *Corophium*
Sand-hopper *Talitrus saltator*
Sandpiper, purple *Calidris maritima*
Scallop, great *Pecten maximus*
  queen *Chlamys opercularis*
Scoter, common *Melanitta nigra*
Sea-beet *Beta maritima*
Sea blite *Suaeda maritima*
Sea cabbage *Brassica oleracea*
Sea holly *Eryngium maritimum*
Sea-kale *Crambe maritima*
Sea potato *Echinocardium cordatum*

Sea slater *Ligia oceanica*
Sea urchin *Echinus esculentus*
Seal, common *Phoca vitulina*
  grey *Halichoerus grypus*
Sedge, sand *Carex arrenaria*
Shag *Phalacrocorax aristotelis*
Shark, basking *Cetorhinus maximus*
  blue *Prionace glauca*
  porbeagle *Lamna nasus*
Shearwater, Manx *Puffinus puffinus*
Shelduck *Tadorna tadorna*
Shell, peppery furrow *Scrobicularia plana*
Shipworm *Teredo sp.*
Shrew, Scilly *Sorex suaveolens*
Snail, violet sea *Ianthina janthina*
Spider, jumping *Tibellus maritimus*
Spoonbill *Platalea leucorodia*
Sprat *Sprattus sprattus*
Spurdog *Squatus acanthias*
Squid, common *Loligo forbesi*
Starfish, burrowing *Astropecten irregularis*
  common *Asterias rubens*
Stonechat *Saxicola torquata*
Stonecrop *Sedum sp.*
Swan, mute *Cygnus olor*

Teal *Anas crecca*
Tellin, Baltic *Macoma balthica*
Tern, arctic *Sterna paradisaea*
  common *Sterna hirundo*
  little *Sterna albifrons*
  sandwich *Sterna sandvicensis*
Thrift *Armeria maritima*
Toad, natterjack *Bufo calamita*
Tope *Galeorhinus galeus*
Turbot *Scophthalmus maximus*
Turnstone *Arenaria interpres*

Vole, Orkney *Microtus arvalis*
  Skomer *Clethrionomys glareolus (Skomer)*

Wagtail, pied *Motacilla alba*
Weever *Trachinus vipera*
Whale, pilot *Globicephala melaena*
Whelk, common *Buccinum undatum*
  dog *Nucella lapillus*
  netted dog *Nassarius reticulatus*
Whimbrel *Numenius phaeopus*
Wigeon *Anas penelope*
Wrack, bladder *Fucus vesiculosus*
  channelled *Pelvetia canaliculata*
  knotted *Ascophyllum nodosum*
  serrated *Fucus serratus*
  spiral *Fucus spiralis*
  sugary *Laminaria saccharina*
Wrasse *Labrus bergylta*

Index

Page numbers in *italic* refer to line drawings, in **bold** type to colour photographs.